C000259749

THE STORY OF
SITTINGBOURNE AND MILTON REGIS

JOHN CLANCY

SUTTON PUBLISHING

First published in the United Kingdom in 2002 by
Sutton Publishing Limited · Phoenix Mill
Thrupp · Stroud · Gloucestershire · GL5 2BU

Copyright © John Clancy, 2002

All rights reserved. No part of this publication may be reproduced, stored in a retrieval system, or transmitted, in any form, or by any means, electronic, mechanical, photocopying, recording or otherwise, without the prior permission of the publisher and copyright holder.

John Clancy has asserted the moral right to be identified as the author of this work.

British Library Cataloguing in Publication Data
A catalogue record for this book is available from the British Library.

ISBN 0-7509-2984-7

Endpapers, front: Men working in the machine shop at Bowater *(Bowater Paper Organisation Ltd).* *Back:* One of Lloyd's early steam-driven tugs with its tall funnel at one of the quays on Milton Creek. *(Sittingbourne Heritage Museum)*

Typeset in 10.5/14pt Galliard.
Typesetting and origination by
Sutton Publishing Limited.
Printed and bound in England by
J.H. Haynes & Co. Ltd, Sparkford.

Contents

Introduction

At the beginning of the twenty-first century Sittingbourne is a much larger place than it was 100 years ago and more. Then it was a small town in its own right, but since amalgamating with Milton Regis and Murston, it's become a large conurbation that's part of the civic administrative district of northern Kent known as Swale. Each area has contributed enormously to make Sittingbourne the town it now is.

Of the three areas, Milton Regis is by far the older, and until the early nineteenth century was the most important. Originally called Middletun, it was the middle town of the kings of Kent and continued to be part of their royal demesne until 1635. The town owes its development and prosperity to Milton Creek, a navigable inlet of the Swale, which separates the Isle of Sheppey from the mainland. Milton reached the height of its importance between the fifteenth and eighteenth centuries as a market town and a port, but it was Sittingbourne's rapid rise during the nineteenth-century industrial expansion that started the decline in Milton's influence, bringing the two towns together.

Murston predates to Saxon times, and from then until 1845–50 was a scattered parish with three manors, around each of which were farmhouses with cottages for the workers. Unlike other more traditional villages, Murston had no central focal point. The only grouping to give any idea of it being a village was around the church and Murston Manor. Its population numbered dozens rather than hundreds. By 1841 the population had risen from 50 in the days of Queen Elizabeth I to 167, but at the height of its importance as a centre for brickmaking and cement manufacture from 1841 to 1870 it grew to over 1,000. Like Milton on the opposite bank, Murston also grew, largely because of its position on the Creek.

Sittingbourne itself is a ribbon development along the old Roman road, Watling Street, spreading east and west from the crossroads that's now Bell Road, Crown Quay Lane, East Street and the High Street. The town's one-street layout proved to be a distinct disadvantage when it petitioned Queen Elizabeth I to hold a market. Before the nineteenth century the High Street would not have been as long as it is now with most of the buildings standing roughly between West Lane and Central Avenue. Except for the inns, most were private dwellings from which business was conducted. None had shop windows as we know them today, although some may well have had stalls outside. Large chain stores did not exist. The Co-op for example, which started in 1874, was an early type of chain store. It had premises in East Street but did not come to the High Street until well into the twentieth century.

Watling Street, linking London to the Channel ports, was the most important road in Kent for many years; it determined Sittingbourne's development and prosperity. The south-east of England has long been the gateway to Europe, and anyone landing at Dover has to travel along Watling Street to get to London. For this reason, Sittingbourne has had a colourful past, playing host to a number of royal personages, nobility, revolutionaries and leading politicians. Being equidistant between London and Dover makes it a perfect overnight stopping place on the journey. In 1697 the celebrated horseback traveller Celia Fiennes wrote, 'This is a very good town for the road and travellers as you shall meet with', and even further back in time, in 1546, John Leland told Henry VIII that 'Sittingburn, alias Sidingbourne, is a prety thorowfare of one parish and by the church renneth a little burne or rille whereof peradventure the towne toke name'.

Sittingbourne was a small hamlet of no importance, except as a way station for the Roman legions, until the murder of Archbishop Thomas Becket in 1170. A steady stream of pilgrims started making the journey to and from his tomb in Canterbury cathedral, and inns and hostelries sprang up to accommodate them overnight. Situated at the head of Milton Creek, it gave commercial traffic ready access to the Medway Towns, London and the continent, which proved invaluable for later industrial development.

The town has never been known for the quality or beauty of its architecture, but its more impressive buildings, once occupied by the wealthier citizens, are generally found on the south side of the High Street. If a business were conducted from the premises, it would be from the front of the property overlooking the High Street. It would have been far more pleasant for the private accommodation at the rear to overlook the open fields and countryside to the south, rather than the industrial creekside area to the north.

The High Street might have been more attractive had it not been for the older Georgian buildings being spoilt by the later addition of unsympathetic modern shop fronts. Fortunately a few do survive intact and for that we must be grateful.

The best architecture can be found in Milton Regis where the High Street consists of many cream-washed, half-timbered buildings, but even here some have been spoilt. Following the Great Fire of London in 1665 brick became a more fashionable building material and many older half-timbered buildings were refaced in brick. Several of Milton's older buildings were treated in this way. But not all is what it may first seem. Look carefully at no. 71, for example. The grey bricks are not bricks at all but mathematical tiles made to resemble bricks. It was a way of avoiding paying the Brick

Tax. At the heart of the High Street conservation area stands the fifteenth-century Court Hall, Milton's one time civic centre.

In the past fifty years a large number of houses have been built in the Sittingbourne area on the agricultural land that once separated the three main settlements from the neighbouring villages of Bapchild, Tunstall, Borden and Kemsley, so these villages can also now be considered as being an integral part of Sittingbourne. While some of this housing development resulted from slum clearance in certain parts of the town, it also brought a new role for Sittingbourne; it became a dormitory town for commuters working in London. The electrification of the London to Kent Coast railway line in the 1960s introduced a fast, frequent train service and boosted the town's population ten-fold.

Subsequent chapters will explore the history and development of each of the three areas that now form Sittingbourne, while others will examine the development of certain trades and industries from which its inhabitants have prospered.

Acknowledgements

In compiling this book, I wanted to present as accurate a picture as possible about the origins and history of Sittingbourne and the surrounding area, which is greatly helped by the use of photographs, postcards and other illustrations. For this I am indebted to the following for their help and input and to whom I would like to record my sincerest thanks: Barry Kinnersley (my main photographer who, despite my often obscure requests, always comes up trumps without complaining); Mick Clancy (my long-suffering brother who in the course of this and my earlier book, was often sent on wild goose chases on his trusty bicycle and came back with some very useful photographs); *East Kent Gazette*; Court Hall Museum; John W. Brown of Local History Publications; Mrs B. Gregory; Mrs J. Halligan (whose collection of cuttings about Milton's past is a never-ending source of reference for me); Fleur de Lis Heritage Centre, Faversham; Mr R. Preston; Ms Lesley Feakes and Geerings Publishers; Mr Wheatcroft; Mr Sage; Sittingbourne Heritage Centre; Mr D. Allen; Mr M. Moore; Bennett Opie Ltd; Mr J. Calvert; Mike Smith; Clive Eglinton of Chalkwell Coaches; David Colthup; Syliva Hankin; *Kent Messenger*; Sittingbourne Library; British Library; Richard-Hugh Perks; Swale Borough Council; Lafarge Cement.

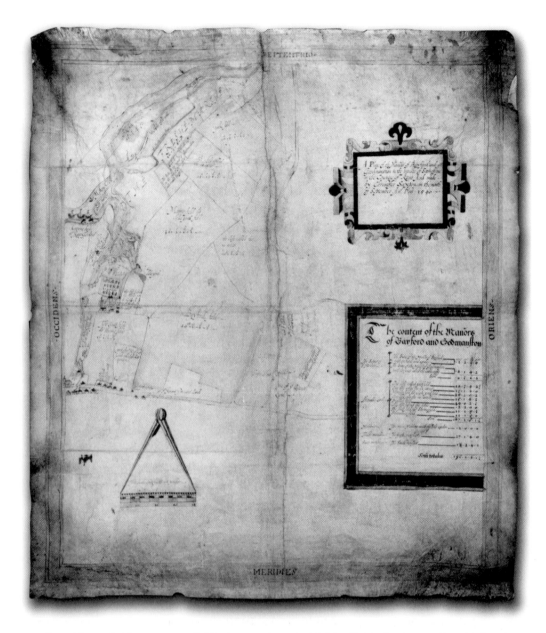

One of the earliest known maps of Sittingbourne, drawn in 1590 by Christopher Saxton. *(British Library)*

ONE

The History of Sittingbourne

It is difficult to know with which of the three areas that make up the town we know today – Sittingbourne, Milton Regis or Murston – we should begin. Each is equally important to the overall development of what we now regard as Sittingbourne as a whole. I'm tempted to begin with Milton Regis, as it's by far the oldest of the three, is the most senior and for many years was the most important. The whole area was a part of the Hundred of Milton; Sittingbourne and Murston did not exist as separate entities. But we'll start with Sittingbourne, as it's now the centre of our district.

The origins of the name Sittingbourne have been lost with the passing of time, but there are a number of possibilities from which to choose, each of which is quite plausible, but equally, none of which can be fully substantiated. In the late fifteenth and early sixteenth centuries there were two different spellings, Sydyngborn and Sythingborn. At this time illiteracy was common and there was no standardised spelling, so the word could have quite easily been mis-spelt. It probably stemmed from this being an area of land once occupied by a tribe called Sything or Sydyng. Some spellings are written as 'Sydingasborn', which makes more sense. The first part of the word refers to the name of the leader of the tribe, 'ingas' derives from the Jutish word meaning 'at the place of' and a bourne is, of course, a stream. There were three such streams crossing Watling Street here.

The most obvious one is that which flowed down Bell Road and Crown Quay Lane and is now below ground in a culvert. When the cinema on the corner of the High Street and Crown Quay Lane was built in the 1930s it was built over the watercourse with disastrous results whenever there was a heavy downpour of rain. As a small boy, I remember the area in front of the stage regularly getting flooded. This is why the Odeon, unlike other cinemas in the group, never had an organ installed. Another stream flowed to the west of the town and came down Ufton Lane and Cockleshell Walk, now one end of St Michael's Road, before flowing into Milton Creek. This one later served our paper mill. The third rose at Chalkwell and on its way to the Creek supported several watermills and tanneries.

Alternatively the name may have derived from the Anglo-Saxon word Saething, which translates into a seething or babbling brook. One other theory suggested by Judith Glover in her book *The Place Names of Kent* gives the name as Saedingaburne, an Anglo-Saxon word meaning the stream of the slope dwellers, endorsed by the *Oxford Dictionary of Placenames* that spells the word as Sidingeburn – once again, very plausible. One other theory worthy of consideration is that put forward by Canon Scott Robertson who in writing *Sittingbourne, and the Names of Land and Houses in or near it: Their Origin and History* in 1879, suggested the town name was more commonly written as Sedyngburne in the Middle Ages. He suggests the first part of the word refers to the tribal name of those who lived here, the Soedingas.

Local legend suggests the name came from the pilgrims travelling to and from Canterbury who stopped at the stream to bathe their aching feet, hence they were 'sitting by the bourne'. If it were so, what was the hamlet called prior to the pilgrims passing through? The same legend also suggests the village of Bapchild got its name from being the place where the pilgrims baptised their children while en route to Canterbury. The site was named Beckett's spring. Once again fanciful thinking, I fear. Bapchild is an ancient settlement whose earlier name was Baccancelde. Whichever explanation you choose to accept, it would appear that the stream is the governing factor.

The Early Settlements

Many towns and cities date to Roman times, and although Sittingbourne is not a Roman town as such, it was a small way station where the legions would rest overnight before continuing their journey to Rochester, or Durobrivae, their next major stopping point. It would logically follow that itinerant trades people would gather here to serve the Romans' needs, selling them pots and pans, repairing their leatherwear and saddles, repairing damaged armour and selling them fish and oysters, a great Roman favourite. This is how many towns began, as a *vecus*. After the Romans left Britain some of these people might have settled in this area and in some cases we know they did. The invading army consisted of some 20,000 Roman troops and about the same number of auxiliaries who were not necessarily Roman citizens. After completing twenty years service these auxiliaries were promised full Roman citizenship and a grant of land where they could settle. Sittingbourne's population could have developed from a mix of Romans, settlers from outside the area and local tribesmen.

Before this period, however, archaeological evidence shows that there was one or more settlements here in both the Iron Age and the Bronze Age at the very least. An Iron Age cemetery was discovered at Highsted in 1955, and in 1928 a Bronze Age axe was found in Ruins Barn Road. Several gold coins bearing the head of King Cunobeline, a British pre-Roman monarch, were unearthed at Tunstall in 1874. It is

Highsted Valley. *(J. Clancy)*

said Tunstall takes its name from Celtic origins and was originally spelt Dunstall, 'dun' signifying a stronghold or fortress, which must have once stood there.

Amateur archaeologist Lesley Feakes has long held the theory that there was a significant sized settlement, possibly of the Iron Age period, at Woodstock in the Highsted Valley. Her theory stems from the Highsted dig of 1955. After walking the Woodstock area over a period of several years when she noticed many man-made earth banks and ditches, Lesley undertook a couple of small exploratory digs in 1996 and 1998. Her theory and finds are expanded upon in her book *Woodstock: An Archaeological Mystery*. There must be many similar sites throughout Swale, and unlike those in urban areas those in the rural districts are gradually being destroyed by ploughing and tree roots.

The Roman Influence

It's not until the Roman period that more tangible evidence exists of occupation in what is now central Sittingbourne. There were two exploratory invasions of Britain in 55 and 54 BC by Julius Caesar who despite spirited resistance soon conquered the south-eastern part of England up to the River Thames. For the next hundred years or so this area remained a client kingdom of Rome, an arrangement that suited most of the local tribes well.

A full-scale invasion under Aulus Plautius took place in AD 43 and Britain became a Roman Province with an occupying army and a provincial administration. After establishing his beachhead at Richborough where he built a substantial castle and port facility, Aulus Plautius struck out, firstly to Canterbury and then on towards London and the north of England, building Watling Street as he went. The line of this road took it straight through Sittingbourne. Great importance was attached to good communications for military purposes and Watling Street became their main artery. The Romans often gave names to parts of their roads and it's said that Keycol Hill and Key Street were named in this way. Keycol derives from the Latin *Caii collis*, the hill (or col) of Caius (Julius Caesar); Key Street stems from *Caii stratum* (or street). However, the old Kentish dialect word 'Key' often signifies the location of a wharf (or 'quay') and it should be remembered that the hamlet of Key Street once stood on a stream that flowed down the Stockbury Valley, across Watling Street towards the Meades and Milton beyond.

Archaeologists have discovered the sites of many villas on either side of Watling Street as it passes through Swale, particularly on the northern side. One of the more important sites was at Boxted Farm between Newington and Lower Halstow, where in 1882 a section of Roman tessellated pavement was discovered. The walls of the building were nearly 200 ft long and were 23 ft wide. They still bore the remains of brightly painted frescos and were clearly once the home of a wealthy citizen.

The villa-farmsteads were laid out in a typically Roman symmetrical fashion close to freshwater streams or springs, and were linked to Watling Street by short, straight roads. The greatest contrast to this occurs on the southern side of the road where the agricultural plain gives way to the heavily wooded North Downs. At that time the Downs and the Weald of Kent were part of the ancient Forest of Blean; it was a most inhospitable environment which travellers kept well clear of.

Over a period of many years several Roman sites have been located and many exciting artefacts have been found, from individual items to sizeable cemeteries, which shows that the Romans settled here and enjoyed a good lifestyle. Many valuable finds were unfortunately either lost or destroyed in the mid-nineteenth century when Sittingbourne's brickmaking industry began. Large areas of topsoil were dug away for the brick-earth beneath and in the process many artefacts were unearthed. The science of archaeology was in its infancy, so there was no question of work being held up while the site was inspected and recorded. If the find looked interesting and valuable the workman pocketed it to sell later; if it was not appealing, he threw it aside. This is how the original site of the town of Milton was destroyed and lost.

We owe a great debt to George Payne, a member of the Sittingbourne banking family Vallance and Payne. George was interested in archaeology and sought to preserve as many of these finds as possible. As new sites were unearthed, George was often to be found on site as early as 4 a.m. awaiting the arrival of the workmen.

In 1869 George reported the find of a highly decorated Roman lead coffin. He wrote to the owner of the land, George Smeed, asking for permission to preserve it, but before his letter was delivered, the coffin had been smelted down as the lead was of the finest quality; it was used to seal the joints of newly laid gas mains in Sittingbourne High Street. Such was the regard for antiquity in the nineteenth century. George Payne was keen to donate all his finds to the town. He made his offer to the Board of Guardians, the former town council, but after careful consideration they rejected it, as it could not afford to provide a proper museum and maintain it. As a result Sittingbourne lost an almost unique collection of artefacts.

The Half-Mile Path in Highsted Road, the only remaining section of the original drove road from Kingsdown to Milton Market. (M. Clancy)

While there have been extensive finds from different periods in history throughout Sittingbourne and Milton Regis, there has not been any evidence of any substantial ancient buildings in the urban area. The position of identified sites does however have some significance. Under Roman law, burial within the town was not allowed so you would expect to find burial sites outside, but close to, residential areas. It was a common Roman practice to bury their dead beside roads so that passing travellers could pay their respects. The location of these gravesites is invaluable in pinpointing the route of a road.

This is highlighted by the discovery of seventeen Iron Age Belgic skeletons in a quarry at Highsted in 1955. The dig revealed much, but no further investigations were conducted at the site and quarrying quickly recommenced. It shows that even then there was a road leading out of Sittingbourne and up the Highsted Valley. This drove road, now Highsted Road, would have connected Kingsdown with the town of Milton, and a short section of it remains as the Half-Mile path running along the side of Highsted school.

Much of the North Downs was heavily wooded, but by the twelfth century was gradually being cleared to form pastures. Local settlements were named from this, so we have, for example, Highsted, a high pasture, on the ancient drove road to Kingsdown, the King's pasture.

Part of the moat that once ran around Bayford Castle in Crown Quay Lane. *(M. Clancy)*

The Dark Ages

The Romans began to withdraw their troops from Britain in AD 410, and after nearly 400 years of Roman rule the country was divided up into several small kingdoms, each ruled by a local warlord. It was a time of great unrest and Britain fell prey to many different foreign tribes.

Little evidence survives of what was happening in Sittingbourne between the departure of the Romans and the arrival of William the Conqueror in 1066, as in the rest of the country, but the area was still occupied.

When St Augustine arrived in Kent in AD 597, he is reputed to have baptised 10,000 people in the Swale, including Ethelbert of Kent, the Bretwalda or most powerful ruler of England. By AD 600 the Anglo-Saxons had conquered most of England. Evidence of their occupation of Sittingbourne can be traced from some seventh-century graves discovered on land to the west of Milton Creek in 1824. There were ten graves altogether, mostly the kind used by prosperous yeoman farmers, but two of them contained a skeleton with a shield boss and dagger, while a third contained a female skeleton with a considerable amount of jewellery. Nearby some Roman graves were discovered, but that's not surprising as quite often the Anglo-Saxons used the burial grounds of their predecessors for their own purposes.

In 1869 a second Anglo-Saxon cemetery was discovered in a field on what was then known as the Rondeau Estate, formerly the property of the Misses Rondeau. The field was bounded on the south side by the London Road and on the west by the garden of Evans's Tannery. Between 1869 and 1871 twenty skeletons were exhumed, and in 1880 another six were discovered on the London Road side of the field. This field with its adjoining properties of Milton House, Albion House and Pemberton House was long ago built upon without the site having been excavated for brick-earth, so no doubt there are many graves laying undisturbed beneath existing properties, awaiting discovery. This is an area, which has changed radically in a short space of time, but I believe is now bounded by Hawthorn Road, Hollybank Hill and Chalkwell Road. The main building of Evans's Tannery still survives as a private house on the corner of Chalkwell Road and London Road. The tannery itself was burned down.

Sittingbourne's oldest church, St Michael's, is said to have been built on the site of the original Saxon church, as happened in Milton Regis and elsewhere. This would seem plausible, but in the eleventh century, when Archbishop Lanfranc set up the Rural

Bayford Court manor house, one of Sittingbourne's original manors. *(Barry Kinnersley)*

Deaneries, there was no mention of Sittingbourne, but then it was part of Milton anyway. Originally St Michael's consisted only of a Norman nave and chancel. A tower at the western end was added later.

At first the church was appropriated to the Benedictine nunnery of Clerkenwell and remained part of its revenue until the Dissolution in the reign of Henry VIII. The church then became Crown property until Queen Elizabeth I granted it to Archbishop Parker and it became a part of the archbishopric. The church was badly damaged by fire in July 1762 when a plumber by the name of Sherwin and other workmen were repairing the lead roof over the south aisle. There was a high wind blowing and when they went off for their lunch they left their fire burning and unattended. Within an hour the whole of the roof had been destroyed and the main body of the church gutted. Fortunately the damage was not as bad as had originally been thought and in the following December architect George Dance reported that the structure could be rebuilt at a reasonable cost.

In the period leading up to 1844 the lady chapel and transept had been boarded off from the rest of the church and used as a school. The pupils were taught to write with their fingers in trays of sand. It was also here that the Archdeacon's Court was held. After the boarding had been removed, the area was cleared out and one of the smaller aisle windows was restored and decorated.

The next major upheaval the country was to face was the Viking raids that according to the *Anglo-Saxon Chronicles* began in AD 893. One raiding party came ashore at Milton Regis. In retaliation, it is said, King Alfred marched his troops towards Sittingbourne and built Bayford Castle on the opposite bank of the Creek about a mile away, to stop any further incursions, but there is no evidence of any truth in this story. Bayford Castle is not to be confused with the manor house, Bayford Court, which stood a short distance away, nearer to the town, and was in the eleventh century the home of Earl Godwin, the father of King Harold. Of Bayford Castle, nothing now remains; it has long been lost in an industrial estate development.

The Norman Conquest

After defeating King Harold's army at Battle in Sussex in 1066, William moved up the coast to Dover to take its castle, after which he marched on to Canterbury where he received the submission of the men of Kent. From there, London was his next target and to get there he must have passed through Sittingbourne. He was to be the first of many future monarchs to pass through the town. Once crowned one of William's first tasks was to compile the *Domesday Book*, a survey of the value of the land, towns and cities he now ruled. Sittingbourne was not included as it was a part of the Hundred of Milton. Following the defeat of King Harold, William punished Harold's noblemen by

Sittingbourne High Street from the air, 1920. St Michael's church can be seen bottom right, the railway station top right. *(Aerofilms)*

declaring them traitors, and seizing their estates and possessions and distributing them among his own loyal followers. William made his brother, Bishop Odo of Bayeux, the Earl of Kent, among many other titles, and granted him the castle and manor of Tonge, which stood on the west bank of Tonge Pond. Today only a small mound topped by a bungalow remains.

The Beginnings of the Town

Sittingbourne started to develop in the late twelfth century following the death of Archbishop Thomas Becket, when a steady stream of pilgrims began to make the long pilgrimage from London to Canterbury and back. Residents were quick to realise that these people needed overnight accommodation, and gradually some of the larger houses developed into inns and hostelries. This trade later developed into catering for the passing coach trade. Because of its position on the London–Dover road, equidistant between both points, Sittingbourne was a popular overnight resting place for anyone passing through and it became a convenient meeting point for ecclesiastical and business dignitaries. The town was definitely on the up.

An aerial view of the West Street/Hollybank Hill end of town, 1920. *(Aerofilms)*

Civil Unrest

Records surviving from the medieval period show there was considerable local interest and involvement in national events. Despite there not being any form of mass communication, the locals would have kept up to date with current affairs from passing travellers on both the main road and the waterway of Milton Creek and the Swale.

Local residents were involved in Wat Tyler's insurrection against Richard II in 1381, a revolt that followed the introduction of a tax to raise money for a war against France. The peasant army marched on London and demanded changes in the agricultural system, which at that time included serfdom. The 'Presentment of Malefactors who have risen against our Lord King' included William Brown of Bixle (near Bredgar) and John Webbe of Maidstone who slew John Godwot of Borden. It was also reported that John Smyth of Tunstall and some others slew John Tebbe at Canterbury.

It was a time when there was an increasingly unstable royal government, which led to growing anarchy when the people of Kent suffered greatly from the brutality and oppression of local tyrants like Lord Saye and Sele, and his son-in-law Sir William Cromer of Tunstall, Sheriff of Kent. In 1450, angered beyond all reason, John Cade rebelled against the king, Henry VI, and according to the Patent Rolls a substantial number of the local community were involved as well as many from the surrounding agricultural areas. Supporting Cade were Thomas Norden, the innkeeper of the George and Dragon, John Goolde, Richard Grovehurst and John Buntyn of Milton.

The rebels marched on London, and after capturing Saye and Sele, and Cromer, beheaded them both. They returned home and were subsequently pardoned for their crime, but not before 'being paraded before the King, bare-chested and with a noose around their necks'. The incident captured the public's imagination and Shakespeare mentioned Lord Saye, Sir William Cromer, Jack Cade and some of their followers in *Henry VI Part II*. Cromer's execution was also referred to.

Another revolt occurred in 1471, known as Fauconberg's Kentish Rising. The War of the Roses between the Houses of York and Lancaster was raging and Sir Thomas Fauconberg, the bastard son of William Neville, Earl of Kent, and a supporter of the House of Lancaster, landed in Kent with an army of mercenaries in an attempt to rescue the former king, Henry VI, who was imprisoned in the Tower of London. Fauconberg sent a letter, written in Sittingbourne on 8 May 1471, to the Commonalty of the City of London requesting them not to prevent him from entering the city. His request was denied, so Fauconberg and his army attacked London, setting fire to London Bridge. As Edward IV approached, Fauconberg retreated back through Kent towards Sandwich. Edward IV pursued him as far as Canterbury, but when later Henry VI died, still imprisoned in the Tower, Fauconberg surrendered. There are no specific Sittingbourne people mentioned as being among Fauconberg's army, but he must have picked up some locals as he passed through on his way to London.

During the reign of Queen Mary in the 1550s Sir Thomas Wyatt led a doomed Protestant rebellion against the Catholic Queen in a plot to put Elizabeth on the throne, following Mary announcing it was her intention to marry Philip of Spain. He was supported by Sir William Cromer of Tunstall who escaped the scaffold, but was sent to the Tower and had his estates forfeited. Four years later Mary died, Elizabeth succeeded her and she released Sir William. The Manor of Tunstall and the rest of his property were restored to him during the early years of Elizabeth's reign when he became Sheriff of Kent. Another local man named Hornden was also involved in Wyatt's rebellion, but after it was quashed assisted the sheriff by executing prisoners.

Sir William Cromer died in 1598 at the age of sixty-seven and was succeeded by his son, Sir James Cromer, who was the last of the family in the male line. It was he who, during the last years of his life, started to build a new mansion house, but died before its completion. The materials were sold to Sir Robert Vyner who used them to build a house in Lombard Street, London; in the eighteenth century it became the London General Post Office. What remained of Sir James's house slowly fell into a state of dereliction and became known as the Ruins, and the road that passed by them, Ruins Barn Road.

The Sittingbourne Charter of 1599. After discovering it in a strongroom of the local council offices, Cllr Peter Morgan, hon. secretary of Sittingbourne Heritage Museum, arranged for the first page to be translated into modern English and a copy made by the Archives Office of Canterbury Cathedral. Having acquired a window unit from Everest Double Glazing Ltd to protect it, the document is now on display in the museum. *(East Kent Gazette)*

The Town's Continued Growth

By 1566 Sittingbourne had 88 inhabited houses, 300 communicants and 2 quays on the Creek, Crown and Holdredge, used mainly for the export of corn and wood. The townspeople thought their town important enough to be granted some sort of official status, so when Elizabeth I visited in September 1573 they made an approach. She granted them incorporation, a weekly market and two annual fairs, but the town gained little from these privileges. Incorporation gave a limited degree of self-government and the right to raise revenue through a rating system, but Sir William Cromer quashed it with physical violence and intimidation. The people of Milton protested against the market and fairs, saying they would be detrimental to their own ancient privileges. It all came to nothing and a state decree of court revoked the grant of the market and fair. Not to be outdone, the townspeople made another application some years later, and in 1599 Sittingbourne was granted a second charter, but only the fairs continued.

> *Elizabeth, by the grace of God, Queen of England, France and Ireland, defender of the faith. To all those present, letters shall come, greetings.*
>
> *As the inhabitants of the town and parish of Sittingbourne in the county of Kent, being in great ruin and decay, have most humbly beseeched us for help and assistance and relief from the great burdens and expenses which they bear from time to time . . . by receiving and lodging in the houses of the inhabitants . . . many right honorable and worthy men, our ambassadors and couriers . . . by providing horses and other necessary things . . . from the Warden and free tenants of the town . . . they may establish a corporation and create a perpetual succession of suitable and capable persons.*
>
> *We do order . . . that the town and parish of Sittingbourne shall be a free town and parish and that henceforth, in perpetuity, there shall be one mayor, 12 jurats and a corporation, which shall have and hold the government and guidance of the town.*
>
> *We order John Catlet, an honorable man, to be mayor of the inhabitants until the 17th day of November, until a suitable person shall be elected for the town. And further, we order John Catlet, John Allen, Roger Genkyns, Randolph Symons, Robert Netter, Matthew Okeley, George Nokes, Christopher Ffranklyn, Thomas Upton, Henry Scrymbesby, Thomas Hummers, Aaron Stickles, and John Amyes to be the first jurats.*

The Civil War little affected this part of Kent. The main battles were much further north. However, shortly before the execution of Charles I in January 1649 there was a Royalist uprising in Kent. Sir Edward and Sir James Hales of Tunstall signed a petition that was presented to parliament. Sir Edward was chosen as General of a Royalist force of some 5,000–6,000 foot soldiers and 1,000 horsemen. They seized magazines and arms as well as the castles at Queenborough and Dover before marching to Blackheath

A map of Sittingbourne and the surrounding area, *c.* 1798, as published in Hasted's *History of Kent.* *(Local History Publications)*

just outside London. Ten men presented the petition while the rest of the force retired to Rochester. The Earl of Norfolk then replaced Sir Edward as General and he took no further part in the war.

During the Commonwealth, when Oliver Cromwell ruled the country, Sittingbourne was sympathetic towards parliament, but there were a number of locals suspected of being Royalists or Catholics, such as Sir Edward Hales, John Throwling of Milton and Robert Barham and Paul Graunt of Sittingbourne. Sir Edward had close links with the Royal family, and in 1688 attended James II when he left London, taking the Great Seal of England with him, and throwing it into the Thames, before making his way to Hales House, Tunstall, en route to Elmley from where he intended fleeing to France. He was captured off Faversham and taken back to Sittingbourne to await escort to London. Daniel Defoe wrote about the incident and reported that the locals

Sittingbourne High Street at the turn of the century before Central Avenue was constructed. *(E.F.H.)*

Sittingbourne High Street in the 1970s before pedestrianisation. *(Dennis & Sons)*

One of the more impressive buildings still standing in Sittingbourne High Street is Brenchley House, the home of the girls' grammar school for many years. *(Barry Kinnersley)*

roughly manhandled the king, so much so that he was never more apprehensive of his life than he was at that time.

Many years earlier Sittingbourne had escaped the attentions of the Domesday survey, but it did not escape historian Edward Hasted who visited while compiling his *History and Topographical Survey of Kent* between 1788 and 1799. It made little impression on him. He noted that while the parish was slightly above the level of the nearby marshes, it was still in a damp situation, and both the air and the water were not healthy, but it was no better or worse than several of its neighbours. He described the town as standing on a descent to the east with a wide, long street, unpaved, the houses of which were mostly modern, being well built of brick and sashed, the whole having a cheerful aspect. Hasted noted that the town's principal support had always come from the inns and houses for travellers, of which there were several, and he was quick to praise the Rose, premises now occupied by Woolworths and a Wimpey bar, as being the most superb of any throughout the kingdom and the entertainment afforded in it equally so.

Sittingbourne continued for a number of years as a small market town catering for the needs of passing travellers with its inns and hostelries. For much of its history the links between the urban and rural economies remained strong. It was at the centre of a predominantly agricultural area, but underwent a radical change in the early nineteenth century when it began a period of industrial development, and from that point onwards the whole character of Sittingbourne changed completely. It became one of Britain's leading centres for papermaking and brickmaking. All of its natural resources, including Milton Creek, were brought together to great effect and Sittingbourne became a major south-eastern industrial area.

TWO
The History of Milton Regis

Adjoining Sittingbourne is Milton Regis, the origins of whose name is less complicated than Sittingbourne's. Milton, or Middletun as it was originally known, was the middle town of the Kings of Kent and had for many centuries been an administrative area within the Jutish kingdom of Kent. There were six principal Saxon towns in Kent and Milton was one of them. It was situated around the parish church near Milton Creek, an unhealthy place in which to live. Many people suffered from the ague, or marsh fever, a condition brought about by malaria-carrying mosquitoes. After Earl Godwin sacked the town in 1052, burning it to the ground in an act of defiance against the king, Edward the Confessor, it was rebuilt where it stands today. Unknowingly, he did everyone a great favour.

The Earlier Settlements

All traces of the site of the original town were destroyed in the nineteenth century when brick-earth was dug out for brickmaking. The earliest traces of occupation of the area were discovered between 1871 and 1878 when circular pits some 10 ft in diameter and 3 to 4 ft deep were excavated at Grovehurst. Flint weapons of the Celtic period were discovered and it is thought that these pits were probably the foundations of former dwellings.

At the same time six lead coffins were discovered behind Back's House on Milton Hill, again as a result of digging out brick-earth. One had a lid ornamented with a lion's head, denoting the deceased had been wealthy and of high rank. At that time only thirty-six such coffins had been found in the whole of Britain, so the discovery of six at Milton was the largest and most significant find to date. In 1889 a large gold finger ring set with a red cornelian and a winged cupid drawing a two-horse chariot was discovered in Milton, showing the wealth of the Romans living there.

Great Grovehurst Farm, Kemsley. *(M. Clancy)*

Back's House, Milton, named after its seventeenth-century owner, Humfrey Back. In later years it was owned by the Jordan family, who were plumbers and glaziers. To the left is Court House which pre-dates 1540 despite its Georgian façade. It was occupied in 1847 by Stephen Court, owner of Court's Wharf. *(Barry Kinnersley)*

Milton's Roman Villa

While most Roman villa sites have been located along the route of Watling Street, there is evidence that one lies beneath Holy Trinity's churchyard. When it was extended to include part of the adjoining field to the north, in 1872, a considerable amount of Roman brickwork and pottery was unearthed each time a new grave was dug. The sexton reported these discoveries to Mr Parham, a master at the National School in Milton. He mentioned it to the noted archaeologist George Payne, who applied to the Kent Archaeological Society for funding to enable him to open a small exploratory trench to ascertain what lay beneath. Money was granted but unfortunately the vicar, the Revd William Harker, would not give his permission for the excavation to take place. No doubt he had good reasons for preventing it, but his selfish action deprived future generations of valuable information about the history of the original town, and the early foundation of the church. The churchyard is now well filled with graves and it is no longer possible to conduct any sort of archaeological survey therein. George Payne gave a full report of the finds unearthed in *Collectia Cantiana* published in 1893.

Local historian Sydney Nicholls surmised there was a substantial Roman villa on the site, judging by the considerable amount of Roman bricks used in the building of the original church. When the church was restored in 1889 and the floor relaid, the foundations of an even older building extending through the south wall and out into the churchyard was discovered. Like those along the north wall, these were also thought to be of Roman origin. Mr Nicholls felt that a Roman altar might be found close to the south door, but he was not allowed to prove his theory.

Part of Halstow church, showing Roman bricks in among the flints. *(M. Clancy)*

While most reports of what might lay beneath the churchyard point to a Roman villa, it could also be a temple. The early Christians tended to build their churches on existing religious sites, and the Romans in turn built theirs on former pagan sites, whereas the Victorians built their churches where the need arose. There are several reasons why this site could be a temple. The fact that the Saxons built their church here is the main indication. However, temples had many roles. They were built near main roads so that passing travellers could stop and pray for a safe journey. According to Sydney Twist, an amateur historian, there was a major Roman road passing through Milton. Temples were also meeting places and a certain amount of hospitality could be offered to those in need. This was where the original town of Milton lay, so it would be far more likely to find a temple here than a villa. In his book on the history of Murston, Sidney Twist suggests there was once a Roman road linking the fortresses at Reculver and Rochester. This is examined in greater detail in chapter three, but if such a road existed it would have passed close by this villa or temple site.

The Saxon Period

During the Dark Ages, when the Saxons ruled the south-east of England, it is believed that the Saxon kings had a palace in Milton Regis, but if this were so, any remaining traces of it would have disappeared when the town site was destroyed in the nineteenth century. Some said it might have been at Castle Rough where the Vikings built their

Holy Trinity church, Milton Regis, c. 1855, as sketched by C.J. Greenwood. *(J. Clancy)*

Milton church. *(Local History Publications)*

stronghold. With no remaining evidence, it can neither be proved nor discounted. However, the surviving church is of Saxon origin. In AD 680 Queen Sexburga of Kent, the first abbess of Minster-in-Sheppey and second abbess of Ely after her sister Ethelreda, is said to have died in its doorway. That doorway is not where the present one is located but where the tower now stands. While most early antiquarians have all said that Sexburga 'gave her life' or 'died' in the door of the church, there is another interpretation of the story we should consider. Sexburga became a nun and when taking holy orders you are said to be 'giving your life to the church, God or Christ'. In those days many services and ceremonies were conducted in the church doorway, much like baptism still is. Could this be what those early antiquarians were referring to? The Saxon church would have been much smaller and simpler than the present one, and would have been mostly destroyed with the rest of the town in 1052. The north wall is all that remains of that earlier church and a small section has been left unplastered, exposing the Roman brick and rough flint construction beneath, typical of a Saxon church.

Holy Trinity Church

The church is one of the most historic and beautiful churches in Kent with a tower said to be the largest of its kind in the county and third largest in England. It was enlarged in the fourteenth century when the porch and tower were added. In the following century a chapel was built for use by the de Northwodes, a notable family in the area, and in 1889, after a long period of neglect, was sympathetically restored by W.L. Grant of Sittingbourne. It is dedicated to the Holy Trinity, a name that could not have been used until sometime after AD 828 when Pope Gregory IV instituted Trinity Sunday. During restoration work in 1917 Sydney Nicholls uncovered two consecration crosses, one at the entrance inside the porch marking the consecration of the south aisle, and another at the western entrance at the base of the tower. These dedications no doubt refer to the rebuilt church of 1070, not the earlier Saxon building.

Because the church was situated so far from the town, it was decided in 1859 to build another nearer the town centre. The numbers of people attending Holy Trinity had fallen drastically and the church had fallen into a state of acute disrepair. It was a gloomy and frightening place to walk past. Ghost stories abounded and the locals avoided it. It was on the verge of being demolished, but towards the end of the nineteenth century Queen Victoria ordered many churches to be restored. Milton's was one of them. The old box pews were taken out and replaced by the present ones; the tower screen was removed; new stained glass was put in the east window; and the communion rail was installed.

The new church, St Paul's, was built in Water Lane, later renamed St Paul's Street, on a piece of swampy ground on the bank of the Periwinkle stream, given by the Archbishop of Canterbury. Money to pay for the building work was raised by public subscription and work commenced in 1863. The builder was George Chrisfield, who built it of local bricks in a Gothic style, typical of the time. It had no pretensions to architectural beauty and its style was described as nondescript. Its rear, overlooking the Periwinkle stream, was more attractive than its front with a large Gothic window set in an apse. The large front doors opened directly on to the street and let in the cold air. It had seating for 700 and was lit by gaslight. St Paul's was demolished in the late 1960s after lying empty and derelict for many years. Today all traces of it and the Periwinkle stream have disappeared under modern industrial units.

The Viking Invasion

The Vikings landed at Milton in AD 893 and built a fortress at the mouth of the Creek, a site now known as Castle Rough at Kemsley. It was to be a base for Haesten's invasion of Kent. Haesten had a fleet of eighty longships, and when you consider each

The site of the Viking fortress, Castle Rough, Kemsley. *(M. Clancy)*

vessel could have held up to forty seasoned warriors, you can see this was no lightning raid or skirmish. In retaliation it is said King Alfred marched his troops to Sittingbourne, erecting a fortress on the opposite bank of the Creek, known as Bayford Castle, from where he could attack the Vikings and prevent them from getting a foothold on this part of Kent but there is no evidence of this.

Castle Rough was only an earth mound and palisade defence structure, so it did not last for many years. When the eighteenth-century historian Edward Hasted visited Milton, he saw the remains of Castle Rough and described it as being 'of a square form, surrounded by a high bank thrown up and has a broad ditch. There is a raised causeway, very plainly to be seen, leading from it towards the seashore'.

In 1972 the Sittingbourne and Swale Archaeological Research Group, under the direction of Ralph Mills, threw doubt on the authenticity of the site. The group excavated the shrub-covered mound, only to unearth fragments of a thirteenth- or fourteenth-century jug and a silver penny from the reign of Henry IV, minted between 1454 and 1460. They concluded that the actual site of the Viking fortress that Hasted had seen almost 200 years earlier was now buried beneath the nearby paper mill. Their

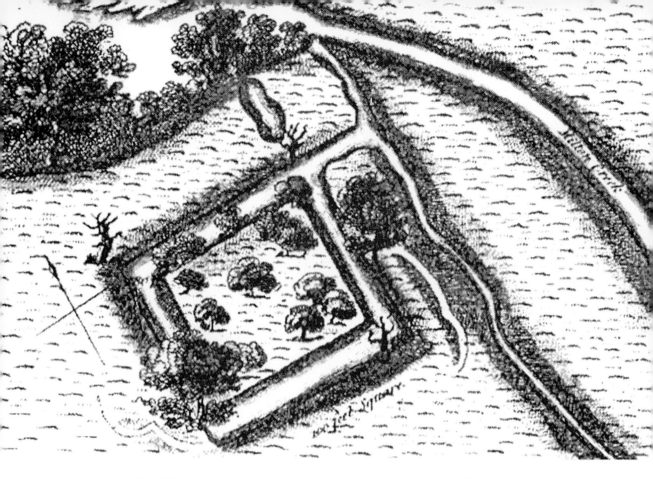

A plan of the Viking fortress, Castle Rough, Kemsley, as seen by historian Edward Hasted, who made a survey of Kent from 1788 to 1799. *(Local History Publications)*

fears were confirmed when both resistivity meter and proton magnetometer surveys proved unsuccessful in locating any underground features or disturbances. Although locals have always regarded Castle Rough as being the site of the Viking fortress, and as such it is still a scheduled ancient monument, when you stand back and look at the site, you can see that it cannot really be so. Without the protection of the sea wall, the area would be flooded, thus enlarging the mouth of the Creek to a size it probably once was, so perhaps the true site really is beneath the paper mill, which is on slightly higher ground.

The Hundred

After the Norman Conquest of 1066 Milton remained a royal favourite until 1635, and as it increased in importance and size as a market town and port, it became the administrative centre for the hundred, known as the Hundred and Manor of Milton and Marden. The hundred consisted of the eighteen surrounding parishes stretching from Rainham in the west, to Tonge in the east, Iwade to the north and Milsted to the south. It also included the Isle of Sheppey, but excluded Harty, which belonged to Faversham, and was annexed to the Wealden village of Marden, covering an area of some 17,000 acres. Of these parishes, Bapchild is thought to be the oldest settlement, being formerly known as Baccancelde with a charter dating from the late seventh or early eighth century. Roman graves were discovered here in 1929 containing coins and potsherds, and in 1953 archaeologists excavated a Romano-British refuse pit containing fragments of first- and second-century pottery. A later excavation in 1972 found even more artefacts, showing that the site was occupied from immediately before the Roman occupation until at least the third century. Tonge was also long-established; its mill is mentioned in the *Domesday Book*. Tonge Castle, next to the mill, was where the kings of Kent called together their councils in the eighth century.

A hundred was the basic territorial unit introduced by the Saxon king Edgar (AD 959–75), who comprehensively revised the law of the land to take into account the enormous changes that had taken place in the previous 100 years. One such measure was the introduction of the Hundred Ordnance. Each hundred was to have a moot, or court, that was to assemble every four weeks to ensure that the king's law was being upheld. It was a highly important measure for the consolidation of local government on a national basis.

The hundred was a sub-division of an area known as a lathe and in Kent there were five full lathes and two half-lathes. Milton was one of the latter but was exceptional in that all other lathes were sub-divided into hundreds. The other half-lathe was Sutton, which consisted of seven hundreds, whereas Milton was also Milton Hundred. It may well be that its unusual status related to its great wealth, which was to continue for a number of years to come. According to a lay subsidy published in 1334/5, north-east Kent, of which Milton was a major part, was assessed at being worth over 20s per square mile. It was the largest area to be assessed at this level in south-east England and was one of the highest levels in the country.

With the Hundred Ordnance as a starting point, Edgar's revised laws were drawn up, 'to be common to all the nation, no-matter whether they be Englishmen, Danes or Britons, in every province of my dominion' and enforced through the boroughs and hundreds as follows:

> . . . *it is my will that every man is to be under surety both within the boroughs and outside the boroughs. And witness is to be appointed for each borough and each hundred. Thirty-six are to be chosen as witness for each borough; 12 for small boroughs and for each hundred, unless you wish for more. Every man is with their witness to buy and sell all goods that he buys and sells, in either a borough or a wapentake [the description of a Hundred under the former Danelaw].*

The Domesday survey (Milton's entry is quoted in full below) valued the Manor of Milton at £200 per year, which made it one of the most valuable towns in Kent. It included 309 villeins, a peasant owing service to the lord of the manor, 74 bordarers, a cottager probably holding a few carucates – one carucate being approximately 65 acres – and 16 ploughs as well as 10 serfs, 6 mills, 27 salt pans and 32 fisheries. The survey referred to a measurement called 'a sulung', which is peculiar to Kent. It originally referred to an area of land that could be worked by one plough team of eight oxen, but by the time of the survey it had become a unit of taxation. The area unit then became the carucate, which was more common in the rest of England. Despite its importance as a central port and market town on a royal demesne, Milton was never a corporate borough.

Terra Regis

In the half lath of Middletune, in Middletune Hundred, King William holds Middeltune. It is taxed at twenty-four sulings; without these there are in demesne four sulings, and there are three carucates in demesne. In this manor there are 309 villeins, with 74 borderers, having 167 carucates. There are 6 mills of thirty shillings and 18 acres of pasture. There are 27 salt pits of 27 shillings. There are 32 fisheries of 22 shillings and 8 pence. Of toll, 40 shillings; of pasture, 13 shillings and 4 pence. Wood for the pannage of 220 hogs; and the tenants of the Weald pay 50 shillings for trappings and horses. In this manor there are 10 servants. In the whole, in the time of King Edward the Confessor, it was worth 200 pounds by tale, and as much when Haimo, the Sheriff, received it, and the like now.

Of this manor, Hugo de Port holds 8 sulings and 1 yoke, which in the time of King Edward the Confessor, were, with the other sulings, at a yearly rent. There he has 3 carucates in demesne.

This land, which Hugo de Port holds, is worth 20 pounds, which were reckoned in the 200 pounds of the whole manor. He who holds Middeltune pays 140 pounds by assay and by weight, and likewise 15 pounds and 6 shillings, all but 2 pence, by tale. The Reeve pays Haimo, the Sheriff, 12 pounds.

Of the King's woods, Wardard has as much as pays 16 pence per annum, and holds half a denne, which in the time of King Edward the Confessor, a certain villein held; and Alnold Cild took away two parts by force from a certain villein.

The Abbot of St Augustine's holds the churches and tithes of this manor, and 40 shillings of the King's, four sulings are payable to him.

Milton's New Town

Following Earl Godwin's destruction of Milton in 1052 it was decided to rebuild the settlement, not on the original site but on a hilltop a mile or two to the south, still

A map of Milton and the surrounding area, *c.* 1798, as published in Hasted's *History of Kent. (Local History Publications)*

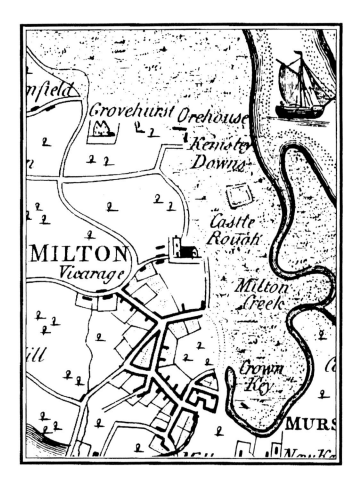

close to the Creek, which gave a sustainable and profitable livelihood. In 1070 work began and it was agreed that the church would be built in a central position on land where the Court Hall now stands. The back lane is still named Cross Lane.

A quaint local legend recalls how after a few days of moving stonework from the old church site to the new something strange happened. Each night the foundation stones that had been laid during the day were mysteriously taken up and returned to their old site. Despite a careful overnight watch being kept on the site it happened several times until a local monk quoted from Psalm 77: 'Except the Lord build the house, they labour in vain that build it.' Clearly it was a sign that the church should remain where it was, and so the new town of Milton had no centrally placed church for many years to come. Our ancestors were superstitious people; it was more likely that someone in a high-ranking position did not want the church moved, but their action had a surprising twist.

In 1989 Bob Risbridger, a founder member of the Milton Regis Society who had spent many years studying the town's history, discovered that the confusion over the resiting of the church led to Milton losing the opportunity to have a cathedral built in the town. It was sited in Canterbury instead. When the location for the new cathedral was being discussed, Milton was much larger and more important than Canterbury, and was more centrally placed. The Saxon cathedral was almost as large as the later Norman building, but many other Saxon cathedrals were quite modest in size. Canterbury's first church, for example, was a wooden structure built by St Augustine in AD 597. It was later burnt down in 1067 and replaced by the magnificent cathedral we have today, but even that evolved over a period of many years. Archbishop Lanfranc commissioned work on the original structure in 1070 and it took seven years to complete. You can imagine the wise clerics and church elders shaking their heads, saying, 'If Milton cannot decide where its own church should be, then what chance do they have of building a cathedral?'

Court Hall

A court hall was built on the land originally earmarked for the church in about 1450 and was used by the lords of the manor as a courthouse. While it has always been accepted that this date is correct, as it has long been painted over the hall's original west-facing door, there's no known documentary evidence to support this. Our only evidence that this is the correct approximate date is the building's method of construction and ornamentation. (However, recent scientific tests carried out on the oldest timbers have confirmed 1450 as a reasonable date for construction of the

Grovehurst Manor House. *(Sittingbourne Library)*

building.) Today we might refer to such buildings as town halls, guildhalls or market halls, but by referring to it as a court hall it better stressed its judicial function. The magistrate's seat and bench can still be seen at the far end of the upper floor and at one time no doubt had a canopy above it.

Originally the building might have had an open-sided ground floor, as many similar buildings of this period still do, and at some point in its history was filled in to form a gaol, a strongroom for the town's valuables and several storerooms, but there's no evidence of this. Outside there would have been some stocks, now long gone, but in a will of 1609 there is mention that Arthur Watt left the sum of 10s for their upkeep. In the same area would have stood a stone market cross, a pump supplying the town with water and a horse trough. Today only a drinking fountain remains.

The building is a good example of a fifteenth-century timber-framed building, and throughout the main part of the original structure wooden pegs were used to secure the joints. Although today the building is in a fine condition, forming the centrepiece of the conservation area and used as a museum, it was very nearly lost.

At first the court hall stood alone as it does now, but over a period of time cottages began to encroach until it was boxed in on three sides. Some of the tenants broke through the eastern wall and used part of the hall's ground floor as their sheds.

Milton's fountain after it was restored by F. Littlewood & Sons, following refurbishment of the High Street in 1998. It was given to the town with a cattle trough by the Metroplitan Drinking Fountain and Cattle Trough Association in 1901. At the outbreak of the Second World War it was removed to the nearby recreation ground to make room for a temporary static water tank. When the High Street was refurbished it was returned to its old position. Across the road is the Three Hats and the White Hart. What became of the cattle trough is not known. *(Barry Kinnersley)*

Two views of the Court Hall, Milton Regis, taken by Sydney Nicholls, soon after he bought it in the 1920s. *(Mrs J. Halligan)*

The rear of the Court Hall, Milton, looking much better than the earlier views taken by Sydney Nicholls in 1926. *(Barry Kinnersley)*

The cottages were demolished in 1956 and the building, by then unstable, was in danger of collapsing. It had not been used since the 1920s when the manorial system was starting to be replaced by a more efficient method of local government, and had been purchased by Sydney Nicholls in 1926 for £75. He restored the building as much as he could and used it partly as a store and partly as a workshop. In 1944 the building was damaged by enemy action during an air raid. Under the guidance of the council's surveyor, Mr Maurice Lashmar, the Ancient Monuments Department of the Ministry of Works soon patched it up. Following Sydney Nicholls's death in November 1945, ownership passed to his son, Arthur, before the hall was sold to Cllr Thomas Buggs. In about 1954 he presented it to Sittingbourne and Milton Regis Urban District Council.

Upon acquiring the medieval building the council consulted Norman Cook, curator of the Guildhall Museum, London, and S.E. Rigold of the Ministry of Public Buildings and Works, who, following a lengthy visit to the dilapidated building, submitted a report on their findings. Capt Jack M. Clarke undertook the recommended work, but no grant towards the costs could be made unless a suitable use for the building could be agreed upon. It was decided to turn it into a museum and W.A. Berry was appointed as custodian. Mr Berry had a keen interest in local history and had helped with the archaeological excavation at Highsted in 1955. Don Allen, clerk to the UDC, had

The newly refurbished Court Hall in Milton High Street, 1999, with its reconstructed roof and end wall using materials from a demolished house in Mill Street. *(Barry Kinnersley)*

obtained one of the skeletons found at the site and offered it to the new museum for display. He also sought loans of items from other local museums and acquired the personal glass collection of Mr L.R.A. Grove, curator of Maidstone Museum. The British Museum donated a copy of the Bredgar coin hoard unearthed by Brian Hollands, and Arthur Nicholls and his sister, Helen, offered several items of local interest. Cllr S.F.J. Forster, chairman of the council, officially opened the museum on 20 May 1959. Following the death of Mr Berry a few years later the museum closed, and remained so until 1972 when the Sittingbourne and Swale Archaeological Research Group took over the care of the museum's exhibits and ran it on behalf of the council. An appeal for funds to run the museum fell upon deaf ears except for one interested local person and property developer Sterling Homes which made a large donation. It was a disappointing start, but at least it secured the future of the museum.

It has often been said that the court hall was under threat of demolition in the 1950s when the surrounding cottages were scheduled to be pulled down. This is not so, according to Mr Allen; it applied only to the cottages, which were in a clearance area. When the cottage at the southern end of the hall was demolished it was discovered that when it had been built, part of the first floor and roof of the hall had been destroyed, so they had to be reconstructed. The roofline from the opposite end was copied to give the building a symmetry and a door and window were added to the new wall, though it is almost certain that there was no door or window there before. The window used came from a demolished house in Mill Street. Those who remember Mill Street might think this a strange place from which to salvage a window for a medieval court hall, but

At the start of the 2000 season, Mrs Gillian Murray, daughter of the late Capt Jack Clarke who some forty-two years ago had done a lot of restoration work to the Court Hall, was invited to unveil a display depicting the story of the restoration project. *Back row:* Don Allen, Cllr Bob Baxter (chairman of the museum) and Keith Chisman (hon. secretary of the museum). *Front row:* Mrs Gillian Murray, Cllr Ann McLean (mayor of Swale). *(East Kent Gazette)*

The undercroft of the Court Hall, Milton, now used as an exhibition area. This was the area the owners of the once adjoining cottages used as their sheds. *(Swale Borough Council)*

The portreeve's official bushel measure presented after much legal wrangling over ownership to the town council by Milton's lord of the manor, Mr H.W. Wykeham Musgrave. Made of bell metal, the measure weighs 73 lb and is 10 in high, 1 ft 8¾ in wide and 7¾ in deep. It is dated 1560 and bears the royal arms of Queen Elizabeth I in red and gold (see below). There is a similar measure in Maidstone Museum, but that only dates from 1601. (Original photographs S. Nicholls, published courtesy of Mrs J. Halligan)

although faced in brickwork, beneath 34 Mill Street was a very old building of two different phases of construction. Its architectural details suggested it dated to around the second quarter of the sixteenth century. Once all the old cottages had been cleared away the area was landscaped with grass and the millstones from Meade windmill set into the paving. Before this was done Mr D.A. Ponton excavated the area, revealing a flint-cobbled surface, beneath which were traces of Anglo-Saxon burials, perhaps part of a much larger cemetery site.

In 1999 the whole of Milton High Street was refurbished, including the area around the court hall. The grass areas were paved over and two sets of the millstones taken up and moved to the Periwinkle mill restoration site in Church Street. With the work completed a reception was held in the hall in April 2001 when Mrs Gillian Murray, daughter of the late Capt Jack Clarke, unveiled a panel commemorating his restoration work. Sadly Capt Clarke had died just a few weeks before the ceremony was due to take place. Also present at the reception were Don Allen and several members of the Nicholls family as well as myself. Unfortunately, many of the earlier exhibits had been removed and handed over to other local museums.

In its 550-year history the court hall has had many uses. In the seventeenth century it was used as a school, and during the Commonwealth Sir Michael Livesey, Bart, who lived in the old rectory at Eastchurch, solemnised marriages there. Livesey was a signatory to the warrant ordering the execution of Charles I and was branded a regicide. With the restoration of the monarchy under Charles II in 1661, the king's magistrates once again presided in the hall.

The Portreeve

The court hall's original function was three-fold. Apart from courts dealing with criminal proceedings held every third Thursday, civil courts were also held, such as the Court Baron where manorial rents were collected annually on 25 July, as well as electing the portreeve and other town officers. The Court Leet was held in October every three years when quitrents, a rent paid in lieu of feudal services, were paid to the lord of the manor.

Court Leet and Court Baron
Official Proclamation
All persons who have anything to do at this Court Leet and Court Baron of Aubrey Herbert Wykeham-Musgrave, Esq., Lord of the Manor of Milton, let them come forward and save their Fines.
(Call the Jury list over and swear them in)
(To the Foreman)
You, as Foreman of this Jury, shall true presentment make of all such matters and things as shall be given you in Charge according to the best of your knowledge. So help you God.
(To the Jury)
The same Oath which your Foreman has taken to observe and keep on his part you and each of you shall well and truly observe and keep on your parts. So help you God.
All persons that have anything to do at this Court Leet may depart hence and give their attendance again on a fresh Summons.

The office of portreeve dates to Saxon times when the monarch derived part of his income from his royal estates scattered throughout the kingdom. The king's representatives on each estate were known as the king's reeves, but where there was a port they became known as portreeves.

Milton was at the centre of a royal estate and King Alfred put its control in the hands of a portreeve elected by those inhabitants of the parish who paid church and poor rates. He was a combination of mayor, market inspector and harbour master. He exercised some of the functions of a mayor in mercantile and day-to-day affairs, but territorial jurisdiction was handled by a manorial steward at a court held at Easter and Michaelmas. He was responsible for maintaining law and order in the town, controlling all the goods that came into the port, overseeing the market and executing the office of the clerk of the market within the hundred of Milton and Marden. He alone set the price of everything that came into the quays or any other Creek within the hundred. Until the beginning of the nineteenth century he was entitled to a proportion of the dues paid on imported coal, which amounted to 4*d* per bushel, the measuring cauldron for which is now in the Court Hall museum. He had an assistant known as the borsholder.

A newspaper report of the portreeve election proceedings in 1836 described the whole business as a complete farce as there was nothing left for a portreeve to do. The old manorial system had been superseded. But, despite this negative attitude, under the watchful eye of the lady of the town, manor and Hundred of Milton, the Right Honourable Sophia Elizabeth, Baroness Wenham of Thame Park, Oxford, and the steward of the court hall, James Taylor, two candidates presented themselves as candidates for election. A similar newspaper report of 1920 shows the election was still being held, overseen by the court bailiff, Mr H.S. Knowles, with Mr A.H. Filmer representing the steward of the lord of the manor. Mr Sidney Nicholls was re-elected as portreeve. The ancient office was abolished soon after, so he was the last portreeve of Milton, serving from 1918 until 1927.

In the mid-1990s the Milton Regis Society decided to revive the title of portreeve and at their annual Saffron Fair, a recreation of Milton's old medieval fairs, elected local newsagent Martyn Gregory to the post. His role is to act as spokesman for the town. Many towns have revived the position of town crier, but this is the first instance I know of the portreeve being revived. Milton used to have a town crier, the last of whom was Edward Knowles.

The symbol of Milton Regis, the wyvern, featured above the door of the old library in the High Street. (M. Clancy)

Milton High Street showing its splendid town hall, later replaced by the library. The town hall was built in 1803 and replaced the old market building that once stood in the centre of the road where the two boys are standing. *(Court Hall Museum)*

Milton's Wyvern

Another popular misconception relates to the symbol of Milton Regis, the mythical winged beast akin to a dragon known as a wyvern. It's been suggested the town adopted this symbol in 1610 when James I granted the manor to Philip Herbert, Earl of Montgomery, whose family crest includes a wyvern, but as this is a Welsh family you would expect it. The wyvern is featured on many sites throughout Swale, and is not exclusive to Milton. It's more likely that the wyvern, being a Saxon symbol, was adopted by Miltonians to commemorate Harold of Wessex, the last Saxon king of England. It might well have been adopted as a defiant gesture against the new Norman overlords.

The Market

Isabella, wife of Edward II, granted Milton the right to hold a weekly market in 1319. She also granted an annual three-day fair, beginning on 24 July (13 July until the calendar was altered in 1751), but by 1878 it had ceased as it was no longer popular.

Milton High Street with the old George Inn on the left. The archway once led to the stable yard, but now it leads to a residential development known as Cortlands. *(Court Hall Museum)*

Milton reached the height of its importance as a market town and a port serving a wide area between the fifteenth and eighteenth centuries. Gradually the town started to grow and spread down the hill towards the Creek where numerous wharves and quays were established. In the reign of Elizabeth I there were 130 inhabited houses, 4 quays, and 26 ships and other vessels. By the late eighteenth century, when Edward Hasted surveyed Kent, the number of houses in the town had increased to 230 and the population to 1,200. Milton was an independent customs port until 1670 with outports at Conyer, Upchurch, Rainham and Otterham.

The market place, or shambles (derived from 'shamels', a word meaning a portable stall) stood in the centre of the High Street by Thomas Bradbury's house, now nos 68 to 72, where there was once a market cross and clock house containing a bell, rung not only to announce the opening of the market but also to call people to church for funerals and parish meetings. The bell was cast at Borden in 1631, unlike most church bells, which were cast at Whitechapel in London. After the clock house was demolished in 1803 the clock was built into the new market building that stood on the site of the former library until 1939. To celebrate Queen Victoria's Jubilee in 1887 a new clock incorporating the original Milton Bell was erected in what was by then the town hall.

From the centre of the High Street the market stretched back down Crown Alley, now known as Crown Road, where there was always a large choice of fresh meat on sale as this was a farming area. This was where people did their weekly shopping. Many other goods were also available; the fifteenth-century will of William Maas refers to his two fish shamels and two tanner shamels.

As market centres, Milton and Sittingbourne were at the economic heart of the hundred, selling produce from the surrounding agricultural parishes. In the countryside nearly two-thirds of the population were employed in agriculture in some form or other. Of the two towns, Milton's market was the more important.

By the sixteenth century Milton and Sittingbourne were very different in terms of status. It was a time when many towns, including Sittingbourne, received charters of incorporation. As the most important manor of the hundred Milton was unquestionably the judicial and administrative centre of the whole area. Whereas Milton's economy was based on its market and manufacturing industries, Sittingbourne relied more on the trade from passing travellers using the main road. By the eighteenth century evidence from burial registers indicates there had been a reversal of roles in the importance of the two towns, a situation strengthened by the early nineteenth century.

A charter was granted to Sittingbourne in 1574 by Elizabeth I, which gave the town the right to hold a weekly market, but following an objection by Sir William Cromer who received part of the tolls from Milton's market, it was revoked in 1579 on the grounds that such a market was prejudicial to that of Milton. The right to hold fairs and a market was reinstated in Sittingbourne's second charter of 1599, but only the fairs continued.

Sittingbourne abandoned its plans to have a market chiefly because Milton was so close and the area could not sustain two markets successfully. It was felt that residents of Sittingbourne could run a stall at Milton market if they wished, and many did. Another factor contributing to the shift of Sittingbourne's market to Milton was the importance Sittingbourne placed on its inns, which required produce in bulk rather than small-scale supplies. A third factor in Sittingbourne abandoning its role as a market town was simply that it was a one-street town, and if it had been cluttered by market stalls the more lucrative coaching trade would have been affected.

Notable Citizens

Thomas Bradbury was a wealthy and influential yeoman farmer, landowner and wool merchant whose name was carved over the oak studded door of his house together with its date of construction, 1586, and the tools of his trade, a pair of sheep shears. When he died in 1601 he left 4 acres of land to the church so that the profits from it could be distributed to the local poor on St Thomas's Day. This later financed the

Hinde House, Milton Regis. *(M. Clancy)*

building and maintenance of seven single-storey almshouses, known as St Thomas's Almshouses, in 1860 at The Butts. Bradbury was not the only benefactor to remember the less fortunate in his will. There were at least eight others, all leaving varying substantial amounts.

Another notable citizen of Milton Regis was John Hinde, who lived in the former manor house on the brow of the hill in the mid-nineteenth century. The tall brick-faced building is of typical Georgian design. Hinde was one of Milton's principal landowners, the town's coroner, clerk to Queenborough town council on the Isle of Sheppey and clerk to the Milton Union. But it was his daughter Eleanor for whom the family is best remembered. She was engaged to be married, but at the last moment her intended jilted her. After her father's death she continued to live in the manor house alone, and in her declining years rarely went outdoors, except at night to visit her father's grave in Milton churchyard. It is said small boys feared passing the house and older ones would knock on the door and run away. She was a recluse and it's been suggested Charles Dickens based his character Miss Havisham in *Great Expectations* on her. Unfortunately the date of the book and the date of Miss Hinde's eccentricity do not tally. She was the last member of the family line and after she died, was interred in the family tomb, which was then sealed up. Ghost stories about the old house abound and local legend tells that the ghost of Granny Hinde can still be seen walking along Milton High Street.

Hinde House was later converted to eight flats, known as Burley's Flats, and was sold in 2001 for £220,000. Mrs Kay Ellis, who lived in one of those flats, spent ten happy years living there. She befriended a lady who lived in a ground-floor flat who told her of a cellar entrance in her floor. It was a stone flag about 3 ft square with a ring in the middle, and she had been told that beneath it was a flight of steps leading to a passageway, which went all the way to Milton church. Whether it's true or not has never been proved, but it could have been an old smugglers' tunnel leading perhaps not to the church but to the bank of the nearby Creek.

Inns and Hostelries

And so Milton grew as a market town with no competition. Sittingbourne's economy continued to flourish on the coaching trade of the seventeenth and eighteenth

The grave of the Hinde family in Milton churchyard. *(M. Clancy)*

centuries, thanks to its position on Watling Street. But Milton also had a coaching inn, the George, at what is now 73 High Street. It was run by George Buggs who was also the town's undertaker and a volunteer fireman. In this latter role George stabled the fire engine's horses in his stables.

Other inns in Milton at this time included the Three Hats and the White Hart, both still serving customers after over 300 years, and the now long-gone Red Lion that operated for about fifty years until 1752. No. 65 was the Crown Inn. The Three Hats was built in 1503 by Thomas Elliott who intended using it as a lodging house. He sold it in 1512 and it wasn't until 1539 that it became a licensed alehouse, its first landlord being Silas Hazeldene. On his death his widow sold the premises to Thomas Snoad, a marine chandler, in 1612. He in turn bequeathed it to his son, Michael, who in 1660 was granted a licence to sell wines. This was when the premises was given the name the Three Hats, a name said to have derived from three cavaliers who dined there at the time of Charles II's restoration.

A token from the Milton Coffee Tavern. *(Court Hall Museum)*

Since then there have been many different owners, but one of the most notable was Thomas Ray, a surgeon and apothecary who as well as running the pub also used it as a doctor's surgery. He later acquired the adjoining property and incorporated it into the inn. This multi-use of the pub continued for the next 100 years with six other surgeons selling ale, wine and medicine, and operating a surgery all at the same time. In recent years it has become just a public house.

These were the principal inns in the High Street, but there were many more common alehouses around the head of the Creek, which gave cause for concern in 1881 about widespread drunkenness. With cheap beer and gin being plentiful and most working-class people living in abject poverty, many sought solace in alcohol. Organisations like the Salvation Army desperately tried to steer people away from the demon drink to a more temperate lifestyle.

Milton Coffee Tavern

One idea was to open a coffee, or temperance, tavern where you could go for a chat, play cards, but not for money, and drink coffee rather than alcohol, and upstairs you could get a bed for the night. It appeared to be the answer. And so on Thursday 27 January 1881 the Milton Coffee Tavern was formally opened by the Revd J.S. Hoare, rural dean, in the absence of the Venerable Archdeacon Harrison who had been taken ill at the last minute.

The Milton Coffee Tavern, believed to have been drawn by the architect W.L. Grant. *(Court Hall Museum)*

It stood at the bottom of Milton Hill on its corner with King Street and had been designed by Sittingbourne architect William Grant who was also responsible for designing the swimming baths, Kemsley paper mill and Gore Court pavilion. The builder was John Seager of Borden. After the opening ceremony 500 people sat down to a tea provided by the steward, John Epps. Afterwards the visitors watched a meeting of the tavern committee.

It had cost £360 to purchase the site, £860 for the builder's contract, £100 for alterations, £150 for furniture and fixings and £50 for conveyancing and the architect's commission. Five hundred and sixty £1 shares had been bought and £50 granted by the Milton Improvement Commissioners, leaving just £890 to be found. However, the Coffee Tavern closed in February 1892 for reasons that are not entirely clear, but it was probably owing to a lack of investment. Either it failed to attract the number of shareholders to keep it running, or it failed to pay off its initial building debts of £890. It was

The reverse of a token from the Milton Coffee Tavern. *(Court Hall Museum)*

reported in a newspaper of the time that takings had dropped to £237 in 1892, whereas in its opening year it had taken £600. Everything possible was done to keep the tavern open, but on 8 March 1892 the company was voluntarily wound up.

Oysters and Fishing

In his survey of Kent the eighteenth-century historian Edward Hasted found 'that for the most part, Milton was inhabited by seafaring persons, fishermen and oyster dredgers'. Burial registers of 1752 to 1757 confirm that nearly all the fishing-related occupations of that time were dredgermen. The oyster dredgermen were an important part of Milton's thriving economy and the Company of Fishermen and Dredgers consisted of 140 freemen who held the lease of the oyster beds at the confluence of the Creek and the Swale from the lord of the manor for £100 and four bushels of oysters annually.

The period leading up to the early nineteenth century had been a time of great change in the economies of Milton and Sittingbourne, a change that had come about through the growth of existing sectors of the economy rather than the introduction of any new ones. Milton was still the main administrative centre of the area and was the larger of the two towns, but it was Sittingbourne that was expanding rapidly.

A Divided Religion

In the mid-eighteenth century the Methodist preacher, John Wesley, came to Sittingbourne to give a lecture on his newly found faith. Methodism became strong in Milton and there were chapels in St Paul's Street and Church Street. A Congregational chapel was also erected in 1790. It was a simple square building with cottage-like windows and folding shutters and was known as the Paradise chapel. Its first minister was the Revd Christopher Muston, who brought Congregationalism to Milton following a series of preachings by the Revd Thomas Wills.

The chapel had an uneventful life until 1856 when the Revd William Parrett was minister. At that time everyone had to pay rates to the Church of England. Many non-conformists objected to this and Mr Parrett took a stand, refusing to pay. His household goods were seized by bailiffs to pay the rate and put up for auction. He only owed 3s 6d, but the over-zealous bailiffs seized goods valued at £6. Non-conformists from Sittingbourne where the rate had been abolished, joined Miltonians in supporting Mr Parrett, and together they bought all the furniture and returned it to the minister together with money to pay his legal costs. As a result of this show of solidarity, the Church rate was abolished in Milton.

In 1860 a new chapel was built on the site of the previous one on the corner of Crown Road and Beechwood Avenue. It was a typically Gothic-style building with a schoolroom and vestry attached. Within three years there were over 300 children attending the Sunday school, so a new schoolroom had to be built. In the 1940s I was one of those children. By 1970 the Sittingbourne and Milton Congregational churches had been amalgamated with a central place of worship in Sittingbourne. Milton's chapel was closed down, and after being deconsecrated became a centre for the Scouting movement. After a fire and being deemed generally unsafe it was demolished in the early 1990s.

Health and Sanitation

Concern was expressed in the mid-nineteenth century about the general state of Milton's sanitation and health. In 1858 a petition was presented to the General Board of Health requesting an inquiry. Twenty years earlier an act of parliament had been passed giving the Milton commissioners the power to raise money by levying a rate or by borrowing money, to pave the streets, construct sewers and drains, provide street lighting, erect privies (outside toilets), remove nightsoil (effluent thrown into the street overnight from bedroom windows), provide public fire engines and prevent nuisances.

At the time of submitting the petition, the streets had only been partially paved by means of lagging, kerbing, channeling and putting down a layer of tarmac. A gas works had been built in 1836 at a cost of £2,000, providing gas for thirty-six street lamps. The gas works was replaced in 1932. During the 1940s and 1950s you could often see a steady stream of people pushing an assortment of wheelbarrows and old prams into the gas works where they could buy coke, a cheap fuel at the time. It was said that if you were suffering from whooping cough you should go to the gas works, as the fumes from it were beneficial.

In the first half of the nineteenth century there was no system of public sewers in any part of the town, so the contents of the privies drained into cesspits, which overflowed into the streets and along the gutters. The smell, especially in hot weather, must have been horrendous. Refuse was dumped in the streets and only partly washed away when it rained. Occasionally it was collected and disposed of properly. The nightsoil and contents of the cesspits was collected by a local farmer about twice a year. Diseases like cholera and typhoid were common.

Milton's first sewer system was completed in 1859, but it discharged untreated waste into the Creek from where many people drew their water supply. A report in 1870 condemned the lack of proper sewage treatment saying it resulted in more deaths than cholera. But it was not only human waste that was to blame. In 1879 Milton Urban Sanitary Authority passed a byelaw requiring any manure deposited in any open space within a hundred yards of a dwelling house or workshop to be removed within forty-eight hours.

The two towns were at loggerheads over their water supply in 1879. Although the 1870 report had recommended the two towns join together to deal with its proposals, it had not happened. When Sittingbourne opened its water works at Keycol Hill, Milton was forced to buy its water from it. Milton wanted to buy an equal share but Sittingbourne was not interested. A local government commission was set up to investigate the dispute and they decided that the three local boards, Sittingbourne, Milton and Rural, should not unite. Sittingbourne was to keep control of the Keycol Hill site and Milton was to pay half of the cost of erecting the works and laying the mains to the junction with their pipes, plus a third of the annual working expenses in return for the right to a water supply in perpetuity. In 1896 the Keycol Hill works were enlarged, but bitterness between the two towns continued. Milton refused to meet Sittingbourne Council to discuss the question of the water and sewage disposal. It was not until 1906 that Milton finally got its own water works at Highsted. It had two wells, each 102 ft deep, excavated by hand. The work had cost £12,800 with a further 10s 4d a day to provide water for the 6,000–7,000 population.

Milton had by the nineteenth century extended right down to the banks of the Creek, an area that constantly suffered from flooding. Little could be done about the problem because of the low lying land and it continued for the next 100 years or so. As a young lad growing up in Milton in the 1950s, I can recall the floodwater stretching back from the Creek, up St Paul's Street (formerly named Water Lane) to Crown Road where my grandparents lived. As Sittingbourne began to grow in the nineteenth century, with new roads being constructed, the two towns slowly began to merge into one. Taking responsibility for the construction and maintenance of roads was no light matter for the council. Their upkeep could be both difficult and expensive.

Civic Improvements

By the nineteenth century the court hall had become inadequate for the town's needs. A new town hall was needed and in 1886 the council adapted the former market building that had been built in 1803. In 1870 the lower part of the building was substantially rebuilt and the front and sides restuccoed. Part of the ground floor, formerly used as a fruit and vegetable store, was converted into a meeting room in 1886.

An attempt was made in 1902 to amalgamate Milton with Sittingbourne, but it failed because of a vigorous campaign to 'Keep Milton for the Miltonians'. Milton suffered from an identity crisis, sharing its name with at least twenty other towns in Britain. Despite adding 'next to Sittingbourne' to the postal address, letters continued

A royal visit to Milton Regis on 14 July 1921 by the Duke of York, later George VI. As well as visiting Milton, the Duke also visited Burley's brickfield and Lloyd's paper mill. He had lunch at Whitehall in Bell Road, the home of Mr and Mrs G.H. Dean. *(Mr Sage)*

to go astray. In 1907 Milton Council decided to change its name to Milton Royal in recognition of its past royal connections. When it formally applied to the county council to make the change, the town council was told the Secretary of State could not sanction the use of the word 'Royal'. Instead they offered the alternative 'Regis', which means of or belonging to the king. It was accepted in November of that year and approved by the county council. Milton was now Milton Regis.

As the town hall was fast becoming unsuitable for modern-day local government needs, Milton Regis Council began looking for a new site in 1926. Their old premises had been condemned, so they turned to the old tannery at Chalkwell and Westfield in London Road, but before any decision could be taken another proposal to amalgamate Milton with Sittingbourne was put forward. It had many points in its favour, and although it was clear that the two towns had once been separate and distinctly different, they now constituted one town. The way the boundary between the two towns divided streets and even houses, caused significant problems, not least in supplying water and sewage disposal. Some streets had two or more sewers and water mains, and both towns went to considerable expense to pump sewage to their respective sewage works, which could without cost drain easily into the others. It was clearly inefficient to have two councils, two town halls, two fire brigades, and so on

The view up Milton Hill towards Hinde House, or Burley's flats, with Back's House in the centre. *(Sketch by David Colthup)*

when one would suffice. Furthermore, if united, their joint size would give them greater status than they would each have on their own.

Sittingbourne Council accepted the proposal and invited Milton Council to a meeting to discuss it further. A referendum was held in Milton with 783 voting in favour of the amalgamation; 1,384 voted against it. Two years later it was decided that the two towns would amalgamate under the name of Sittingbourne and Milton Regis Urban District Council, Sittingbourne having objected to the original choice of Milton Regis and Sittingbourne. Next to go was the Rural District Council of Milton Regis, which merged with that of Faversham in 1934 to eventually form Swale Rural District Council. Milton Regis had now lost its own individual identity and had become the poor relation of Sittingbourne.

THREE
The History of Murston

The third parish, which together with Milton Regis constitutes the town of Sittingbourne, is Murston, the name of which is said to have derived from mors tun or marsh town. Like its neighbours, Murston dates to Saxon times, and is, unfortunately, the least historically interesting part of our town. However, despite that it played a major part in the development of the area as a whole. Although it is a village in every sense of the word, it has never had a village centre. It has long been a scattered parish with three manors and farmhouses with adjacent workers' cottages.

Situated on the eastern bank of Milton Creek, like its neighbour Milton, it was until the mid-nineteenth century an unhealthy place in which to live. In his *History of Kent*, published in 1829, W.H. Ireland told how the air was impregnated with fog, which hovered about 3 or 4 ft over the ground, emitting a most noxious smell, and when combined with the badness of the water, gave the inhabitants severe agues. After several years' exposure to this they developed a yellowish complexion.

Another historian, Dr Plot, observed in 1688 that seldom did any of the natives live beyond the age of twenty-one, an observation mentioned in a rhyme in Will Lambarde's *Perambulations of Kent* in 1570 when he said: 'He that will not live long, let him live in Murston, Teynham or Tonge.'

Unlike Milton it had no cause to relocate and stayed as a country parish with good, rich farming land and oyster fisheries until the mid-nineteenth century when it became an industrial centre producing bricks and cement. Its population exploded from 50 in the days of Queen Elizabeth I to nearly 1,000 in its heyday between 1841 and 1870.

The parish boundaries remained unchanged from when Honorius, Archbishop of Canterbury, first divided the diocese into parishes in AD 636, until 1950 when the newly developed area of Snipeshill was included. It runs broadly from the banks of the Swale back to just beyond the A2 road and from the Creek across to Tonge and Bapchild.

East Hall, one of Murston's original manor houses. *(M. Clancy)*

Merescourt, another of the original three manor houses of Murston. *(M. Clancy)*

Notable Buildings

In 1841 there were only twenty-five houses in the entire parish and they included the three manor houses (Murston Court, East Hall and Meres Court), the Rectory, Tracey House in Tonge Road, the Golden Ball public house (then a small farm), two cottages opposite the stables (now a social club), two cottages where the Co-op stands, the farmhouse and two cottages at Murston Forstal, two more at Little Murston farm, three at the Ferry Inn, Elmley and a fifteenth-century cottage at Four Oaks.

Murston's manorial boundaries have long been swallowed up by land development. The manor house of Murston Court once stood opposite the old church in Gas Road, and after a long and illustrious history, having been owned by some notable local families, was demolished in about 1880. Nos 18–20 Gas Road were built on the site in 1882, but they were demolished in 1963, so if you once lived at any of these addresses, you had history beneath your feet.

The largest of the manor houses was the fifteenth-century East Hall with its magnificent tithe barn from the same period. The manorial rights attached to it were first granted in the reign of Henry III (1227–72).

Meeres Court was once described as a capital mansion, and before being sold to Smeed Dean for part of their industrial development programme for Murston, had been occupied by several notable local families. It was the smallest of the three manors.

Still standing in Tonge Road is Tracey House, now called Murston House. Until 1890 the road had been called Tracey Lane. This fine example of an early Georgian house was once the home of Dr J.M. Tracey MD, who died in 1845 aged sixty-six and is buried in the old churchyard.

Another interesting old building is the Golden Ball public house. The original part of this building dates to 1650–1700 when it was a small farm of about 10 acres. The farm was known as the Golden Ball orchard and was bought by Smeed Dean in 1890 except for 1 acre, which was retained by the owner. The former farmhouse was turned into a beer house in the 1840s and a taproom was added. Domestic rooms were added in 1920 and a clubroom in 1930.

Murston House, formerly Tracey House, one of Murston's oldest properties. *(M. Clancy)*

The Golden Ball public house, formerly the Golden Ball orchard farmhouse. *(M. Clancy)*

Elmley Ferry

Murston was an important place in the nineteenth century, as the ferry to Elmley from the village was one of only three crossing points to the Isle of Sheppey. In 1847 charges were 3*d* per passenger, 6*d* for a man and horse, 1*d* per head for horned cattle, and 4*d* per score for sheep. There was a coastguard cutter stationed nearby at the mouth of the Creek with a crew of one officer and four men. Smuggling was rife in this deserted corner of Sittingbourne and there are still many footpaths leading from Elmley Ferry back to the main road that were once used by the smugglers.

An enchanting story recalls that in 1842–3 the excise men heard that some contraband was being unloaded at Adelaide Dock, a favourite haunt for smugglers. Acting on a tip-off, they went to the house of the horsekeeper of Muggleton's brickfield and searched the premises for the contraband. Unfortunately they were too late and found nothing. The lady of the house was sitting on a stool nursing a bad toothache. Her long skirt was draped around the stool and the excise men didn't like to disturb her. What they failed to notice was that the stool she was sitting on was actually the last barrel of brandy the smugglers had been unable to get away before the excise men had arrived.

In 1847 Elmley, on the Sheppey side of the crossing, had a population of forty-two with seven houses. By the 1860s it had expanded to forty houses and had a public house called the Globe, so the ferry was quite important for business. The village also had a cement works that closed in 1904 and a church dedicated to St James, the patron saint of fishermen, which was eventually demolished in 1950. All traces of this village have now gone, but when the sun is low in the sky, if you know where to look, you can still see the platforms on which the buildings once stood.

On the mainland side of the Swale was Elmley Ferry centred round the inn. Built in the seventeenth century, the three-storey weatherboard-clad Ferry House operated as an inn until 1914. The ferry closed in about 1940, but the ferrymen still occupied the accommodation until the floods of 1953 forced them out. The last two remaining ferrymen were Jack Carrier and Jack Wade. Carrier died in the 1940s, and after advertising for a new ferryman the authorities decided that the ferry service was no longer needed. The railway company had built Kingsferry Bridge at Iwade in 1858 and from then on Elmley Ferry's trade began to drop. The inn was the last building to survive, but now even that has gone and nothing remains of this part of Murston, except for the causeway stretching out into the Swale, which can be seen at low tide.

The causeway of Elmley Ferry, the last tangible reminder of the once busy ferry service, with an abandoned vessel rotting on the beach. *(M. Clancy)*

This bungalow is built on the remains of the bailey on which Tonge castle once stood. (M. Clancy)

Tonge

To the east of Murston is the ancient parish of Tonge, marked today by Tonge pond and the old watermill. For many years Tonge Castle overlooked the pond, and today only a small part of the original bailey remains with a modern bungalow built on it. Between 1819 and 1843 there was a windmill on this hillock, owned by John Scott until 1829. His name and the date 1816 were cut into the plaster of an old, disused watermill that stood beside the windmill with which it once ran in conjunction. After these mills were demolished 3 ft of soil was taken from the top of the mound to make a garden in the old millpond of the watermill.

The origins of the castle are most interesting, according to George H. Packer, who at the turn of the twentieth century wrote an essay on the history of Sittingbourne and the surrounding area. In AD 425–58 Vortigern ruled over the largest part of the British kingdoms. To maintain law and order he used mercenaries like the Jutish brothers Hengist and Horsa. However, in about AD 450 the Jutes revolted against Vortigern and founded their own kingdom, in probably what is now Kent. The *Anglo-Saxon Chronicles* record that the Jutish war lasted for some thirty years and forced the British to abandon Kent.

Before the revolt, Vortigern showed his appreciation for the Jutish brothers' defeat of the Scots and Picts by offering them any reward they cared to name. Hengist asked rather modestly for a piece of land that could be encompassed by a single ox hide. It might seem like a trivial request, but if the hide were cut into slender strips, or thongs, it would stretch a long way. This is exactly what Hengist did and it gave him an enclosure large enough upon which to build a castle. It is from these thongs, Packer suggests, that Tonge Castle got its name. Originally it had a moat on three sides and a deep sheer trench cut down on the fourth.

Early Brickmaking

Despite Murston not being the best of places in which to live, because of its unhealthy environment, a dramatic change in the mid-nineteenth century made it the brickmaking centre of this area, adding greatly to Sittingbourne's overall growth and development. The rebuilding programme of Victorian London, brought about by the invention of the railway, created a huge demand for bricks with a high tensile strength, and Murston had all the necessary raw materials needed to make the yellow Kentish Stock brick. It was more durable and much cheaper to make than the traditional red brick. The great brickmaking entrepreneur was George Smeed who began operations in 1846. Within fourteen years he owned rapidly expanding brickfields, shipyards and a fleet of barges. He also built and paid for a gas works at Murston in 1863, which included a 1,000-ton coal store on a wharf that had deep-water collier berths. A gasometer was erected by Cutler and Co. in November of that year and it was connected to Sittingbourne by an 8-in main pipe, providing gas for the town's streetlights at £4 10s per year per lamp. Domestic gas was also supplied to those houses that wanted it, but some people complained to the local newspaper that it was more expensive than that supplied from Milton.

In 1875 George Smeed formed the Smeed Dean Co. with his son-in-law G.H. Dean. Smeed Dean is credited with being responsible for developing Murston into the industrial centre it became in the nineteenth century. George Smeed engaged John Andrews as his brickfield foreman in 1865. He had had little formal schooling, and although he could read, he could not write other than to sign his name. In his younger days he had been a rough character, but he knew how to make bricks and he knew how to handle men. From such beginnings, he rose to become a director and general manager of the works. The Andrews family was an archetypal Victorian family who became prominent citizens of Sittingbourne and Murston. They had deep religious beliefs, self discipline and gladly accepted hard work, all of which they attributed to being at the centre of their success. John's son George was chairman of Sittingbourne Urban District Council from 1913 to 1915.

George W. Smeed, 1812–81. *(Swale Borough Council)*

Between 1860 and 1870 George Smeed built 150 houses for his workers in Lower Murston in an area bounded by Church Road, Gas Road

All that remains of All Saints, Murston's thirteenth-century church. Most of it was demolished in 1873/4 and the materials used to build a new church some distance away. This remaining portion is the original centre chancel. *(Barry Kinnersley)*

and Adelaide Dock. Families like Smeed and Andrews did much to foster the community spirit that developed Murston in the last quarter of the nineteenth century. There were other smaller brickfields like Muggleton's, Askington's and McKenzie's that were making bricks some five to ten years before George Smeed, but they never expanded and were eventually absorbed by Smeed Dean. These early brickmakers are covered in more detail in a later chapter.

The Church

The original church of Murston was situated at the northern end of the village. It was mostly of Early English design and was built in the late twelfth and early thirteenth centuries. It had three chancels, a nave with a transept and a square tower topped with a wooden turret, housing three bells. On the south side there was a large porch. When the Revd James Hoare became rector in 1866 he declared that he didn't like the size or situation of the church, so in 1873 he decided to demolish it and use the materials to build a new church further south at a cost of £3,000. In a newspaper report published shortly before the old church was demolished, Ben Hawkins explained how the old church could only hold 100 worshippers and the parish was growing rapidly. Furthermore, it was in a bad state of disrepair and was considered unsafe. The gas works had recently been built nearby and the fumes emitted from it were noxious to worshippers. The Revd James Hoare was a man with a strong personality who demanded respect from everyone. Any schoolchild who met him in the street had to salute him, and if they failed to do so, would be reported and caned before the whole school. When visiting homes in the parish Hoare would often knock on the door and, without waiting to be invited in, open the door and announce himself.

It's hard now to understand the attitude of our Victorian ancestors, but it should be remembered that they lived in a much harsher environment. They believed in success through personal endeavour and sacrifice, and, through reading the Bible, found the precepts which they saw as leading to a just society, always bearing in mind the adage, 'The Lord helps those who help themselves'. The last service held in the old church was conducted in July 1873, and the new church opened for worship exactly one year later in July 1874. The central chancel of the old church was left intact to serve as a mortuary chapel. Adjoining the new church is a parish hall that has interesting origins. When the idea of having a parish hall was first mooted, it was suggested the money for it should come from donations and a public collection. In 1922 Smeed Dean purchased the old institute (forerunner of today's NAAFI) building from the wartime airfield at Throwley and had it erected beside the church with an adjoining caretaker's house. Smeed Dean paid the wages of the caretaker, who was, for many years, the church sexton, Ben Hawkins. Known as the parish hall up until 1932, Smeed Dean had retained the freehold, so when APCM bought out the company they took over the building, renaming it the Works Welfare Hall. It was later acquired by the Kent County Council.

The Long-Lost Roman Road

In his book *Murston Village and Parish* Sydney Twist expounds the interesting theory that a major Roman road once ran through Murston, in addition to Watling Street, a road already well known. Sydney's suggested road linked the Roman fortress of Reculver at Herne Bay with another at Rochester. Perhaps it was a sort of service road used mainly by the legions travelling from one place to the other and as such it would have been relatively free of other travellers.

When you study the Ordnance Survey map of the area you can see that it could have been a possibility. For much of its route through Herne Bay, Whitstable, Seasalter,

Graveney, Faversham, Teynham and Tonge the road is as straight as the coastline will allow in a typically Roman fashion. It's only when the road gets to Murston and has to cross the Creek that it becomes a little blurred. It is thought that the crossing point might have been at the former Adelaide Dock near the old church, and after crossing the Creek would have continued towards the site of Bayford Castle, along what used to be known as Kidneys Hill, over Crown Quay Lane and thence towards Milton church. From there it would have headed through Bobbing, Upchurch, Lower Rainham, Lower Gillingham, Chatham and then Rochester. The route between Milton and Lower Rainham is not quite so obvious now that much of the land has been used for orchards, but when you draw a line between the Lower Rainham Road and Quinton Road, a pattern starts to emerge.

The theory can be substantiated, as along much of its length there are religious houses and small chapels, which were set up to look after the needs of passing travellers. On either side of the Creek there are Roman burial sites that were placed to remind travellers of the deceased, a typically Roman practice. One is at Murston and the other in Milton, both on the line of the suggested road. It is believed there are the remains of a Roman villa or temple beneath the ground in Milton's churchyard, so this could well have been a point towards which the road would have headed, as this was where the original town of Milton once stood. If further proof were needed, the Romans had a pottery works at Upchurch producing what became known as Upchurchware. Close by, another villa was discovered in Newington. It is certainly food for thought.

From the 1890s onwards the demand for bricks began to fall with serious competition coming from cheaper bricks produced elsewhere. In 1930 the parish council merged with Sittingbourne Urban District Council and the area began to lose its separate identity. Despite this, Murston remained a close-knit community, and even after the merger still considered itself to be a village with all the amenities you'd expect. In 1964–5 all 150 houses in Lower Murston were demolished and the residents moved to the new council estate in the Oak Road area. Much of what was once the old village is now part of a huge industrial trading estate, and there may not be many left who would still say 'I'm proud to be a Murstonian'.

FOUR
Early Trades and Industries

For many years Sittingbourne has been at the centre of an extensive agricultural area known as the Hundred of Milton. Agriculture was the principal occupation of the district with most of the population being engaged in it, either on a farm or in one of its many allied industries. Its long-established practices have had a direct bearing on the nature of our countryside to this day. Much of what was farmed was for home consumption and for sale to local inns and hostelries, but much was exported to London as well. The area was at the forefront of several agricultural revolutions, including one that introduced fruit and hops to Kent.

Sittingbourne is centrally placed geologically on a fertile belt of rich, loamy soil stretching for almost 35 miles from Rainham in the west to Thanet in the east. It averages a width of about 8 miles and supports cereal crops, hops, orchards, market gardens, pastures and woodland. It has long been an area of mixed agricultural practices, and despite significant changes during the nineteenth and twentieth centuries the types found in the hundred have changed little in 2,000 years or more. In the north recent alluvium clay deposits on the marshes are followed by a strip of brick-earth and London clay on either side of the main road, and the older Woolwich and Thanet deposits are overlaid by rich loamy soil, which is ideal for crop growing, and to the extreme south, an upper layer of chalk covered by a flint-strewn silty drift.

The heavy Kentish turn-wrest plough maximised field use, allowing the ploughman to work continuously from one end of the field to the other without a break. The fine loamy soil was continually tilled without being left fallow for a year, as was the earlier practice. The idea of planting root crops like barley, beans and wheat instead of leaving the land fallow was established here. Much of the local cereal crop was sent to London from the quays on Milton Creek, and in 1649, of all the ports in Kent, Milton was second only to Faversham in the quantity of cereal it exported to London. It was one of several ports used by coastal vessels servicing the needs of London's growing population. As London grew in both size and status during the seventeenth century, so too did the economic links between the capital and the Hundred of Milton.

While this was profitable for the landowners, it was not popular with locals when there was a poor harvest. For financial reasons, exporting cereal crops came before local needs. In 1631 there was a bad harvest and fifty or sixty women from Sittingbourne and Milton rioted against this unfair exporting practice. It was but one of many corn riots to happen all over North Kent in that year.

Diversified Agricultural Practices

As it was such a large area with different soil types, there was a wide diversification of different agricultural activities in each of the rural parishes. Murston, Tonge, Bapchild and Rodmersham for example were ideally located to grow corn and other cereals in their uniquely large fields. Whereas the average field size was 18.4 acres, in these parishes it was not unusual to find them measuring 49 acres. Because of this some farms had only two or three fields. Kent was a county characterised by ancient enclosures, and by the sixteenth century some farms had fields of 60 or even 100 acres. In Kent the replacement of the former common field system with the new method of enclosure did not come as a result of enforced enclosure, as had been the case elsewhere in the country, but because of high rents and the high rate of workers' wages. The farmer had to make the best use of his land and joining small fields together seemed like the best option.

The land to the south-east of the hundred – the parishes of Kingsdown, Milsted, Tunstall, Bredgar and Borden – was more heavily wooded, being situated on poor, chalky soil covered with flint stones. Agriculturally it was not the best land on which to grow crops, so the woodland was gradually cleared away to form pastures for livestock. Certain trees in parts of the woods were regarded as a crop. The rents of chestnut woods in the seventeenth century were generally high and coppice wood could be sold to a dealer for around £8 per acre. The timber from the chestnut tree was used to make fencing spiles and posts. In 1575, when Elizabeth I owned the manor of Milton, one of her annual dues was 9 bushels of chestnuts or payment in lieu.

Timber from oak trees growing in the hundred would have been in great demand for ship building, although the main bottom timbers would have come from redundant men o' war being broken up at Sheerness and Chatham. The bark from the oak trees was needed for the tanning industry based in Milton.

Borden was a village surrounded by orchards of fruit trees. The value of orchard land was high compared to arable or pasture land and required less acreage than corn to make a living. The seventeenth-century agricultural reformer Samuel Hartlib suggested that if land were turned over to orchards its value would increase twenty times. He further stated that trees should be planted some 20 or 30 ft apart in rows and the land between then ploughed and sown with corn until the trees began to bear fruit, after which it should be laid down as pasture. He had found that grass in orchards grew two weeks earlier in spring than meadow grass and lasted better in hot dry summers. It also had the added advantage that cattle or sheep kept in the orchard could shelter under the trees.

By the second half of the eighteenth century hop growing was on the increase throughout Kent, despite it being an expensive crop to cultivate and one that was susceptible to bad weather. The high price of hops yielded a better return, and so many orchards were grubbed out and hops planted in their place. The soil in which the fruit trees had been growing was particularly good for the hop plants, leading to high yields. From the mid-seventeenth century Kent had about a third of the hop acreage of the entire country, and most of the crop would have found its way to London. Another benefit of hop growing was that beer brewed with hops lasted much longer than the traditionally brewed ales that only had a shelf life of around three days. As water could not always be guaranteed to be pure, ale was the accepted alternative drink in varying strengths for the different members of each family, as the brewing process made the water safe to drink.

In the Hartlip area there was a long tract of waste ground covered with broom and furze. It was of no agricultural use, but the land, known for many years as Queendown, was a noted warren for rabbits, then known as coneys. Rabbits are not a native animal; they were introduced into this country from Spain in the twelfth century. Like the fallow deer, they were brought here by the Normans but some escaped from the confines of their estates and thrived in the wild. In 1674 landowner Captain Osborne hired William Hallom as his warrener at his home, Queendown Park. The rabbits were used both for their fur and their meat, and even up to the 1950s rabbit was often a traditional Christmas dinner for some. Teynham also had a warrener who monitored the rabbit banks belonging to the lord of the manor. The warrens or 'coney earth' were probably at Conyer, hence the origins of the village's name.

To the north-west of the hundred were those parishes that were situated on the marshy ground, which was clearly of no agricultural use whatsoever, but this didn't stop them from contributing to the hundred's economy. Otterham Creek near Upchurch had a wharf used for the import and export of corn and timber and was a part of the port of Milton. Halstow Creek had oyster beds. During the seventeenth century more cattle were being kept on the marshes when new grasses, like clover, were introduced and used as fodder. At this time in Kent, a herd averaged about 14 beasts, but on the marshes it was nearer 22. This similarly applied to sheep, particularly in the summer months, when a typical flock might number 70 in north Kent, but on the marshes it often grew to as many as 376.

Most of Kent's native cattle at this time would have been the smaller red beasts descended from those brought over by the Anglo-Saxons, and owned by small-scale local farmers. Larger stockbreeders would have black and whites, Welsh runts and

Northern steers, all from the northern counties or Scotland. It was common for cattle drovers to drive their herds down to the cattle fairs or markets held at Canterbury, Maidstone or London, and then stay on to earn some extra money working on the farms during harvest time, and return home in October or November. There are several reports of local farms employing groups of Welshmen.

The land at Iwade was particularly good for keeping sheep on, as it was mostly even, flat and soft. Often wet ground can cause problems for sheep but this never happened in Iwade. Much of the meat from the hundred would have gone to the inns at Sittingbourne, to Milton's market or to the quays for export. As well as mutton, beef and rabbit, there was an abundance of wildfowl caught in a decoy to the north of Milton. These birds were much appreciated for their size and flavour and many were taken to London each week, along with the fleeces and hides that were surplus to local requirements.

Tanning, Leather Goods and Pipe Making

Allied to the meat trade was the tanning industry, which turned animal hides into leather. It was a major industry in Milton where there were two tanneries, both at Chalkwell, then a small, separate hamlet near the main London–Dover road, centred on the tanneries and a couple of watermills. One of the three streams that crossed the main road would have surfaced nearby, having flowed down from Heart's Delight near Borden.

The process was lengthy and the tannic acid used in the process was obtained from the bark of locally grown oak trees. To produce 150 lb of leather, it took 100 lb of hides and 300 lb of oak bark. After the hides had been tanned by soaking in tannic acid, they would have been hung in a drying shed or loft. If dealers did not have sheds they could rent a plot of land, which was kept clear for this purpose, where the hide was stretched out and pegged down with tenter hooks. This gave rise to two expressions: 'on tenterhooks' and 'tan your hide'.

It was a good living renting out a plot of spare land. As well as the tanners, weavers also used them, stretching out their newly woven and washed lengths of cloth on a tanyer frame. If it sounds rather risky to leave leather or cloth on an unattended plot of land, it should be remembered that if someone was caught stealing it was a hanging offence.

In 1862 there were ten separate businesses making boots, shoes, saddles and harness in Milton alone. There were two grades of leather used for saddlery, 'brown', which was uncoloured leather, and a more expensive 'black', which was used for carriage harnesses. Other leather goods that would have been in great demand included holsters, pouches, gun cases, belts, portmanteaux, bags, leggings and satchels.

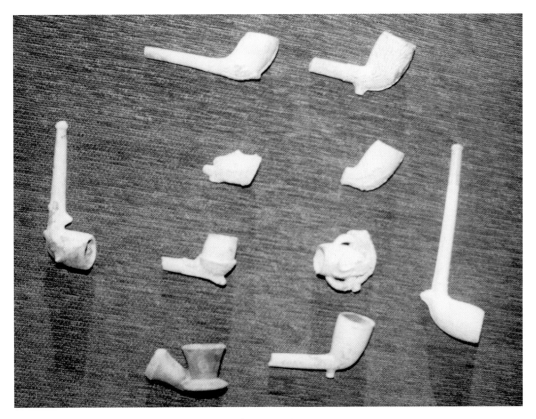

A collection of clay pipes such as those made in Milton. *(M. Clancy)*

Another byproduct from the meat trade was tallow, made from various animal fats, which were melted down to make candles, the standard form of lighting indoors. John Budds was a tallow chandler with premises in Crown Alley, now Crown Road, where it met the High Street. Together with the smell of the tanneries, this formed another of Milton's renowned Seven Stinks, the others being the Dung Wharf, the Creek, the gas works, the sewage works and the fellmongers (dealers in animal hides).

An essential trade in most old towns was pipe making. Tobacco was smoked more in pipes than in cigarettes as was the later fashion at the end of the nineteenth century. On the bank of the Creek stood Flushing Street, a road erased by the modern Mill Way. A local pipe maker by the name of William Webb lived there. The pipes were made of fine, greyish-white clay and were formed in folding metal moulds; the stems were pierced with oiled wire. Because of their delicate nature, they were much in demand and being cheap to buy many people purchased them in bulk. It's been suggested that as many as fifty gross of these pipes could be fired in a kiln in eight or nine hours, and they cost around 7*d* per gross. As they were a very disposable item, it's not uncommon to find broken pipes when digging gardens all over Milton.

Exotic Plants

Two exotic plants grown in Milton at this time were saffron and tobacco. Saffron has been valued for centuries as a spice, food colourant and dye, and was first smuggled into Britain in the fourteenth century. It's a difficult plant to grow and time consuming to harvest, which explains its high price. Saffron is produced from the stigma of the crocus, and was grown for about a hundred years in the Middle Ages in a field on Sprottes Hill, first owned by John Baylie, then Tomass Berrie and later Dennis Bradley, who died in about 1574. There was a great demand for the yellow dye it produced for use in the thriving wool trade. Verification of this trade in saffron comes from the Court Rolls of 1665, which records, 'Anthony Webb acknowledges himself Tent. [tenant] to a Tenm't with the Appurtances at Sprats Hill, Rent at 10*d*. Also Saffron Garden, Rent 5*d*.'

There was also a saffron garden at Teynham as well as a vineyard, which was on the slope below the church, facing east. Incidentally, Teynham was the first place in Britain to grow cherry orchards. Richard Harrys, fruiterer of Henry VIII, planted them in 1533. It established the Kent fruit belt that exists to this day, known as the 'Garden of England'. The continental fashion of eating fruit spread to England in the early sixteenth century, and rather than pay extortionate prices importing fruit from abroad, Henry VIII decided to plant his own orchards. As well as sweet cherries, he also planted Pippin and Reinette apples.

In the nineteenth century it was legal to grow tobacco for medicinal purposes on a plot of land no larger than 40 square yards. Growing it for any other purpose, such as smoking, would have made the grower liable to a fine of £10.

Watermills and Windmills

As the Hundred of Milton was predominantly an agricultural area, milling would have been an important trade. Wind and water were two sources of power upon which Britain depended for centuries. The *Domesday Book* lists six mills at Milton, all of which would have been watermills; our windmills were all built in the early nineteenth century. Except one, the mills were located on the stream that ran from Chalkwell to the Creek. First there was Mede mill near where Bennett Opie's factory now is; then there was Periwinkle mill, used to ground pearl barley and which is currently under restoration; Kings mill was next, to the east of St Paul's Street; and finally there was Tidemill on Milton Creek. Lastly, there was Meades mill, which stood opposite Dingley Close in Vicarage Road. It stood on the stream that had originally flowed down the Stockbury Valley, across the main road at Key Street, into the Meades, then on to Cornford's Lake by Milton church before discharging into the Creek. After falling into

The Meades windmill, Milton Regis, *c.* 1870, typical of the many 'smock mills' that were built throughout Kent at this time. *(Court Hall Museum)*

a state of dereliction, what remained of this mill site was sold to the local council in February 1929 together with 10 perches of land for £135 and developed into a recreation ground. The location of the sixth mill is open to speculation.

Our one remaining watermill, or what's left of it, is the Periwinkle mill. In his survey of Kent, Edward Hasted pointed out the mill was used to produce pearl barley, and it was said to be the only mill in the country where pearl barley was made to the same perfection as that of Holland.

When the mill stopped working it was bought by the Hales family, who ran a butchers there until the 1960s. The mill house had been slowly deteriorating and by 1968 was in such a dangerous condition the owners had to have it demolished. Although the building itself was razed to the ground, much of the mill machinery remained intact. With the owner's consent, the Sittingbourne Society commissioned a firm of conservation consultants to examine the feasibility of restoring the machinery as the central exhibit of a purpose-built museum. It's an on-going project that will take a lot of time and money, but as the area's one remaining watermill, it should be preserved for posterity.

The old Periwinkle mill before demolition in the 1960s. The road running from left to right is Church Street. The stream is that which rose at the junction of Chalkwell Road and London Road. Today only the footpath to the left remains. *(East Kent Gazette)*

The water wheel, all that remains of the Periwinkle mill. It is currently undergoing restoration by members of the Sittingbourne Society. *(Barry Kinnersley)*

Little is now known about these early watermills, which makes it even more important that the Periwinkle mill restoration project succeeds. However, a little is known about the Tidemill, which in Elizabethan times had been known as the Fluddmill. In a sale advertisement dated 1838 it was described as 'a Tide and Steam Mill consisting of a very substantial, first-rate water corn mill of four floors, running four pairs of French stones, with gear-work and machinery capable of grinding and dressing 75 quarters per week, together with a newly erected brick building, with a steam engine of 12hp driving three pairs of French stones and capable of dressing 88 quarters per week'. The advertisement further noted that the situation of the property was one of the best in the county for obtaining wheat or disposing of flour.

Unfortunately by 1861 the tide pool that fed the millrace was giving cause for complaint. A letter to the local newspaper complained that 'the tidal pool, which covers an area of about five or six acres, is, during most of the day, nothing but a mass of mud, sedge and decayed vegetable matter. The stench from it, even in the winter, is at times hardly bearable and forms an excellent hotbed for fever and the ague.' The writer went on to point out that there was more severe fever and typhoid in the area of housing near the tidal pool than in the rest of Sittingbourne and Milton.

After the Meades watermill in Vicarage Road ceased to function it was left derelict for many years, and much of the brickwork and roof tiles was used to build the summer

Standing in Church Street today with your back to the Periwinkle mill site, this is where the stream once flowed beneath the industrial units. The footpath is the original. *(M. Clancy)*

house in the adjoining recreation ground in 1936. What was left was used as a changing room and store for a number of years. Like the other watermills it was used to grind corn into flour. In the early nineteenth century a windmill was built a little further along the road near the railway line; it was used to grind pulses for animal feed.

Sittingbourne and Milton had three windmills between them. Chalkwell mill stood on the south side of the A2 road, close to Borden Lane, and is clearly defined on the OS maps of 1819–43. It was a black smock mill with one floor under the stage and had three pairs of grinding stones. In 1878 and for many years thereabouts the miller was Richard Thomas Snoard, a farmer as well as a miller. The mill was sold for demolition in the 1890s when it became necessary to build houses on the site. The machinery for driving the steam engine, which was never used, was purchased by Milton's millwright, Mr F. Littlewood, who later installed it at Meades mill for John Bates in 1889.

Meades mill was the last windmill left standing. In earlier times it had been owned by George Ride and in about 1860 by his son, J. Ride. It was severely damaged in a gale in 1868 when Mr Ride was injured. The mill was then bought by Mr J. Barnard, who had it substantially repaired in 1878 by millwright Frank Littlewood. John Bates, who had a corn, hay and seed merchant's shop in Milton High Street, was the next owner in 1889, and it was he who had a steam engine and auxiliary underdrive made by Gardiner's of Frederick Street, Sittingbourne, fitted. Unfortunately this improvement led to a tragic accident. Charles Tutt, who had previously worked at Stedman's mill in Gillingham, started work at Meades mill. Soon after starting his new job he was found drowned in the water tank that supplied steam power to the auxiliary engine. The mill ceased working in 1920 and, following a survey by the Society for the Protection of Ancient Buildings in 1930, it was purchased by Milton Regis Urban District Council who boarded up the derelict building. It was struck by lightning in the early 1960s and was subsequently demolished.

Another windmill clearly shown on the OS maps of 1819–43 stood in what is now Hawthorne Road, near its junction with Charlotte Street on the brow of the hill. Like the other two it was a tarred smock and stage mill. It was where the milling family Ride were born and brought up. In 1880, when Mr Harris owned the mill, a steam engine was installed as auxiliary power, a popular move with many millers at the time. By the end of the nineteenth century the mill had become derelict and it later burnt down.

This was the general pattern of trade and industry in the pre-eighteenth century hundred of Milton. Mechanisation, the coming of the railway and improvements in farming methods all played a part in slowly altering the overall picture. Fortunately industrial expansion in the nineteenth century had little effect, as the geological structure of the locality ensured that it was only in the parishes situated on the belt of clay in the north of the hundred that brickmaking developed. Those parishes situated on the chalky soil to the south were not subject to industrial development and were able to continue with their agricultural way of life.

The disused oyster pond at Murston, 1999. Once oyster fishing was a major industry for Miltonians. Their oysters were said to be among the finest in the country, even surpassing the famous Whitstable oysters. Now they have all but gone, the pond is a haven for wildlife. *(J. Clancy)*

Oysters and Fishing

As market centres, albeit in different ways, the two urban parishes of Sittingbourne and Milton were at the economic heart of the hundred as a whole. Milton Creek served both towns and each had their own wharves and quays, but Milton was the centre of the local fishing industry, specialising in oyster dredging. Oysters were once part of our staple diet rather than the delicacy they are now. Archaeological evidence shows this to be so since at least the Bronze Age. Milton's oysters were said to be second to none in the whole of the country, and during the eighteenth century London street traders could often be heard shouting 'Buy my fine Milton oysters'. The finest oysters are produced on a seabed of London clay in clear salt water, and for many years the Swale and Milton Creek provided perfect conditions. The oysters thrived.

Milton's oyster dredging industry dates to the thirteenth century when King John granted the rights to Faversham Abbey. The Milton fishing ground extended from Faversham to Kingsferry and included parts of the mouth of the River Medway known as the Lappel Bank and Stangate Creek. The fishing grounds were clearly defined in legal documents and were jealously guarded. In 1489 there was a dispute between the lords of the manors of Whitstable and Milton, and the Privy Council was called upon to adjudicate. As a result, Milton was awarded further rights at the mouth of the Swale, but with a strict limitation on dredging and with sale only to 'their one market at home or in that quarter of Kent'.

In 1740 the fishermen had to petition the king, as foreign ships being held in quarantine at the mouth of the River Medway were discharging untreated effluent and waste into the sea, contaminating and destroying the oysters. By the nineteenth century the situation had deteriorated even more as the brickmaking industry began to grow. Barges that sailed through the fishing grounds were fouling the area by spilling bricks, brick dust and ooze. The government set up a select committee to investigate the general state of the industry. One major problem they found was that the grounds had been over-dredged, and it was recommended that no dredging should take place in the summer months to allow stocks to re-establish themselves. And so in 1877 a consignment of oysters from Lisbon was laid between Harty and Elmley.

Increased sewage pollution and the development of the paper industry in the twentieth century further added to the demise of the industry. In 1909 the Fishmongers' Company prohibited the sale of all shellfish harvested at Elmley as it was so badly polluted, marking the end of Milton's status as a premier fishing port.

Brewing

Whereas Milton placed great importance on its fishing industry, inns were paramount to Sittingbourne's economy. Many of the innkeepers were also landowners, so they could supply their establishment with produce from their own farms. Many even brewed their own beers and ale.

For a short time both Sittingbourne and Milton had private breweries. Milton's, the Milton Brewery, is remembered in the naming of Brewery Road and stood where Langley House once was. It was established in about 1850 and was acquired by Frederick Leney and Sons Ltd, a company with many business interests, in 1895. The company also purchased public houses when they came on the market. Locally they owned or leased the Shakespeare, New Inn, Forresters Arms, Golden Eagle, Old Oak, Malt Shovel, Britannia, Grapes and the Chalk Tavern, many of which are now long gone.

Sittingbourne's brewery had been established in the reign of James I. By the nineteenth century it was in the hands of H. and O. Vallance in a building that was later to be used as the Queen's cinema. It traded as the Sittingbourne Steam Brewery between 1860 and 1880, before being acquired by Style and Winch Ltd in 1905.

A sign of Sittingbourne's importance as a market town was the livestock market held each Monday behind the Bull Hotel. *(J. Clancy)*

The Shire pub, formerly the Shakespeare Hotel, shown before Gaze Hill Avenue was built opposite in the 1920s. *(J. Clancy)*

Clock Making

Clocks began to be used much more widely in the eighteenth and nineteenth centuries, but it is little known that between 1767 and 1874 there were thirteen clock makers working in Sittingbourne. Whether they made clocks by putting together pre-manufactured components or made those components themselves is not fully known. Their names are recorded as being Edward Acres – 1767, J. Baldwin – 1770, John Chapman Crittenden – 1796, James Bernard – 1800–47, G. Foster – 1802–13, F. Young – 1803, Edward Shilling – 1839, John P. Smith – 1839–47, E.S. Smith – 1851–5, John Blaxland – 1866, A. Baker – 1874, T.W. Taylor – 1874, Jesse Caryer – 1874.

FIVE
Passing Trade

It seems almost inconceivable that a chance malicious comment made by King Henry II about his longstanding friend Thomas Becket should lead to his cold-blooded murder, and greatly affect the future development of Sittingbourne. But that's exactly what happened.

The King and Becket had long been friends, but eventually their relationship deteriorated. After a heated argument Henry was allegedly overheard to say, 'Will no-one rid me of this turbulent priest?' The knights who overheard this sped off to Canterbury, thinking they were doing the king's bidding, and murdered Becket in the cathedral. Stories of miracles happening at his tomb in the crypt soon spread; his blood was said to have miraculous healing powers and the tomb became a shrine. From 1170 onwards visits to Becket's tomb became the most popular pilgrimage in Britain and Western Europe. Many hundreds of pious pilgrims made the journey from Southwark in London (although in those days it was in Surrey) where they congregated at the Tabard Inn, along Watling Street, to Canterbury and back. In 1420 it's recorded that 100,000 pilgrims had visited the shrine.

Sittingbourne's close proximity to Canterbury and its unique position of being almost equidistant between London and the Channel ports, made it an ideal and convenient overnight stopping point on the long journey. To begin with, the town did not have the inns and hostelries to accommodate travellers; they were to come later as a direct result of this passing trade.

The Pilgrims

After the Norman Conquest many religious establishments, such as monasteries, priories and hospitals, were built all over the country. Most were quite small, built close to main roads and were designed to look after the elderly and sick as well as providing overnight accommodation for passing travellers.

Maison Dieu, Ospringe, Faversham, *c.* 1890. The pilgrims passing through Sittingbourne on their way to and from Canterbury could seek overnight accommodation and help from two religious establishments: Swainestry and Schamel. Both buildings have long since been demolished, but a similar one still stands in Ospringe. To the left is a stream flowing off the North Downs towards Faversham Creek in much the same way as those in Sittingbourne once did. *(Faversham Society)*

At that time Sittingbourne was little more than a small hamlet with a few houses grouped around St Michael's church. As travellers approached the town from the west, the first building they came across was the chapel and hermitage of Schamel, dedicated to St Thomas Becket. It stood on the south side of the main road where the Volunteer public house and the Convent school were much later built. Like most religious establishments at that time, it offered accommodation for the weary travellers.

The Schamel hermitage is said to have got its name from a priest named Samuel whose job it was to say mass daily and to attend to the needs of passing pilgrims, in return for which they would make a small donation to the chapel. After he died the building fell into a ruinous state and was later rebuilt by an Augustine monk.

His successor was Walter de Hermestone who was appointed by Eleanor of Provence, queen of Henry III, in 1271. When he arrived to take charge of the chapel he found that the people of Sittingbourne, led by the vicar, Simon de Shordich, had wrecked the building. They had carried off the chapel bell and altar, and installed them in their own church. It is said that soon afterwards, Simon de Shordich died from the effects of the curses showered on him by Walter de Hermestone.

Sixteen years later the queen, who in holding the manor and Hundred of Milton and who was therefore the patron of the chapel, held an inquiry. From those records we learn that a small hamlet known as Sittingbourne Parva existed around the hermitage. The chapel was then again rebuilt and little is known about it until June 1358 when Philippa of Hainault, queen of Edward III passed by and gave 20*s* in alms. A friar by the name of Richard de Lexedon was then in charge of the chapel. Two years later King John of France passed by on his way home and gave a sum of 20 nobles, approximately £120. The hermitage was eventually destroyed in about 1542.

In approaching Sittingbourne from the east, the pilgrims would have come across a similar establishment known as the Hospital of the Holy Cross of Swainestry on the brow of Snipshill where Rectory Road playing field now is. The people of Sittingbourne had completely the opposite attitude towards this establishment than they had towards Schamel. Wealthy tradesmen left considerable sums of money in their wills for its maintenance and for the repair of roads leading to it. Why this difference? Perhaps it was because they thought they could squeeze out of the home-going pilgrims any spare cash they might have as they left the town.

It was not long before some of the townspeople began to realise that a comfortable living could be made from the pilgrims. The accommodation at Schamel and Swainestry was limited and could not cater for everyone, so gradually some of the

St Michael's, Sittingbourne's original church, 1920, that would have stood in the centre of the early Saxon settlement. A niche cut in the buttress which would have held a statue of St Mary, revered by passing pilgrims, can just be seen behind the trees to the right. *(J. Clancy)*

St Michael's church, Sittingbourne, showing the niche where once stood the statue of Our Lady of the Buttress which was worshipped by passing pilgrims. It was held in such high esteem that several parishioners asked to be buried close to the statue itself. It may well have been destroyed during the Reformation. *(Barry Kinnersley)*

larger houses were adapted to take paying guests. The inn was born, which was timely, as by then religious establishments were being dissolved by Henry VIII, and by 1535 most had been destroyed. Elizabeth I gave responsibility for the care of the sick, poor and elderly to the individual parishes.

While in Sittingbourne pilgrims would have paused to hear mass outside St Michael's church. On its south-eastern corner there is a niche cut into the buttress that once held a statue of the Virgin Mary. This statue was held in high regard by locals and there are several instances of them asking to be buried close by. Until 1765 there was a large wooden porch where travellers could rest.

By 1340 Sittingbourne was well established as a principal resting place and is one of the few towns actually mentioned in Chaucer's *Canterbury Tales* in the chapter 'Words Between the Summoner and the Friar'. In recognition of this, the J.D. Wetherspoon pub opened at the end of the 1990s by the corner of the High Street and Bell Road is called The Summoner.

Sittingbourne was not the only place that tried to fleece the pilgrims. As they approached Bapchild a hermit would leap out into the road, asking for alms for his altar at the Leper Hospital of St James of Puckleshall. It's not known exactly when this establishment was founded, but the earliest mention of it is found in the Pipe Roll of 1181–2. This upset the vicar of Bapchild who received nothing from the pilgrims, so he set up his own rather dubious shrine. The exact location of the hospital cannot be verified, as only tantalising clues are left to suggest its whereabouts. *Archaeologia Cantiana*, vol. xix, suggests it was on the north side of The Street but within the parish of Tonge. A stream running down from the Highsted Valley once crossed the road near what is now the Fox and Goose public house on its way to Tonge pond, and St James leper hospital probably stood near it. Nearby were some cottages, at the rear of which rose a spring known as Becket's spring. In 1556 Queen Mary granted the hospital to

Sir John Parot, a knight, but as the hospital had ceased to fulfil its functions some years earlier and had been described by Leland in 1543 as 'being quite down', it's fair to assume what Sir John was actually granted was the land where the former hospital had once stood. The site of the chapel and its adjoining graveyard awaits discovery.

Coaching

The more stable social conditions of the sixteenth century encouraged travel for its own sake. As well as pilgrims, many noblemen with their large retinues of servants and retainers would have also travelled along Watling Street on their way to and from London. Whereas the kings and queens usually stayed in nearby great houses, the local innkeepers did well out of looking after their followers. The accounts of Henry VIII, for example, show that in November 1532 he paid the landlord of the Lion in Sittingbourne the sum of 4*s* 8*d* for overnight accommodation for his servants and followers. The Lion, or Red Lion, is Sittingbourne's oldest inn. The most spectacular of these cavalcades to pass through must surely have been that of Henry VIII and the Hapsburg Emperor, Charles V, in May 1532. They charged John Cheney of Ufton, Sir

The rear of the Red Lion stableyard in Sittingbourne High Street, 1968. *(Sketch by David Colthup)*

The Rose Inn. *(J. Clancy)*

William Cromer of Tunstall and Sir John Northwode of Milton with finding lodgings for their estimated 2,000 followers. In September 1573 Elizabeth I stayed in Tunstall overnight on her way to Canterbury. The elders of the town took the opportunity to petition the queen for their first charter. Elizabeth probably stayed at Grove End, it being the oldest house in Tunstall and for many generations the home of the Cromers.

Hasted reminds us that Sir John Northwode of Milton entertained Henry V at the Red Lion in 1415 on his victorious return from the Battle of Agincourt at a cost of 9*s* 9*d*. Seven years later the king's funeral cortège halted at Sittingbourne on its way from Dover to Westminster while the Bishop of Norwich held a service in the parish church. One of the last royals to stay in the town was the Duchess of Kent with her daughter Princess Victoria and Princess Leopoldine Esterhazy who occupied all of the first-floor rooms of the Rose, our last inn to rise to eminence, in 1825. It had been built in 1708 by Robert Jeffs and in recognition of this royal visit was later renamed the Rose and Victoria. It would seem that most of our monarchs and many from Northern Europe have stopped in Sittingbourne at some time or another during their reign.

Sittingbourne's role as a town offering hospitality to passing travellers was recognised in its second charter of 1599, which referred to the town as 'receiving and lodging . . . and providing horses and other necessary things for many right honourable and worthy men, Ambassadors, couriers and their mounted attendants . . . for which it is most suited . . . by its situation, being at a convenient distance from other places'. This charter was granted, following action taken by the townspeople in 1591 to protect their trade of supplying the needs of travellers.

In the sixteenth century it took five days to cover the 71-mile journey from London to the Kent coast. Overnight stops were made at Dartford, Rochester, Sittingbourne and Canterbury. By the eighteenth century Sittingbourne's geographical position in relation to London affected the economy of the town following a change to faster stagecoaches. By then the Rochester–Sittingbourne–Canterbury–Dover–Deal Flying Stage Coach was leaving London three times a week and covered the journey in only one and a half days with one overnight halt at Sittingbourne. In 1726 George II travelled directly to Sittingbourne from Hythe without making the customary halt at Canterbury.

This was the great age of coach travel, both stage and mail. Sittingbourne's place in Kent's social and commercial life was at its peak. Many countywide meetings were held in its hotels. It was, for example, the place where the county's gentry called a meeting to consider their response to Napoleon's threatened invasion.

The innkeepers played a significant role in the economic well-being of the hundred as a whole right up to the nineteenth century. In 1670 coins were in short supply so Mr Webb of the George Inn issued his own halfpenny tokens. Mr Webb was the local postmaster and Sittingbourne's position on the London–Dover road had led to the town's early development of the postal service. Innkeepers who were also postmasters dealt with more than just mail. They provided a horse and a guide for the next stage, as well as supplying food and accommodation.

The growth of Sittingbourne as a coaching centre in the seventeenth and eighteenth centuries increased the differences between the town and Milton Regis enormously. With numerous inns and hostelries needing produce for both people and their horses, their requirements would have been more for bulk supplies than the small-scale needs of private householders. Many of the inns were supplied either directly by local farmers, who might also own the inn, or through a wholesale system. Sittingbourne was dealing in commodities on a large scale.

The owners of the inns were often local gentry or businessmen, as was the case of the Lushingtons who owned the George Inn, formerly the George and Dragon. They also owned a house in Sittingbourne, had three manors, three farms, orchards, woods and land in the parishes of Sittingbourne, Milton, Rodmersham, Minster and Thurnham, as well as owning the Horn Inn in Sittingbourne, which once stood next door to the Bull where there is now a furniture shop. Their imposing three-storey building in the High Street was extensively remodelled in the early eighteenth century to become their town mansion house. Being one of Sittingbourne's largest inns, it had accommodation for forty pairs of horses at the rear. The Lushingtons often entertained Georges I and II here on their way to and from their lands in Germany; hence, it is said, when the premises reverted to an inn later in the eighteenth century it was renamed the George. The public house to the right of the stable yard entrance was in earlier times the inn's alehouse known as the Bell, a name later given to a new inn called Sweepstakes that stood in East Lane, which in turn became Bell Lane. This probably happened when the Lushingtons converted the George into their home.

Closely linked to the business of innkeeping was that of brewing. Many inns as well as private homes had their own malthouse or brewery attached. In the nineteenth century there were two proper breweries, one in Milton and one in Sittingbourne, but according to a plan of a house dated 1733, there was a sizeable brewhouse situated between the George Inn and the White Hart. This latter inn was where the babywear shop now is and the archway entrance to the rear stable yard can still be seen running along the side of it. The shop to the right, now part of Blundell's furnishers, would also have been a part of it. At the time it was owned by the Tong family who also owned the Horn, the Ship and the Bull alehouse, all High Street inns and hostelries that have since long gone. The structure of John Tong's brewhouse survived well into the twentieth century with the family initials and the date 1753 clearly to be seen in the brickwork.

The End of the Coaching Era

The days of long, exhausting and sometimes dangerous travel by stagecoach were numbered by the invention of the steam engine. By 1858 the railway had come to Sittingbourne, and London could be reached within a matter of hours rather than days. Its position as an overnight resting place was no more. Many of the inns and hostelries managed to stay in business but others failed. Although the advent of the railway led to the decline of the town as a staging point for coaches, it fostered the growth of Sittingbourne as an industrial centre, and the expansion of the commercial functions of the High Street resulted in many shops taking over those buildings previously used as inns serving the coaching trade. The grandest, the Rose, was put to other uses. For a number of years Woolworths has occupied it, but its adjoining alehouse remained as a public house until recent times when it was changed to a Wimpy bar. Lushington's former George and Dragon, later to become his town mansion house, is now Blundell's furnishing shop and only its adjoining alehouse, the George Inn, remains to this day as a public house. The Globe that once stood next to the Horn on the right-hand side of the archway near the Bull became the town's first workhouse and is now a solicitor's office.

As you wander along the High Street today the location of some of those former inns and hostelries becomes obvious, despite their modern shop fronts; many had a carriage archway leading to stables at the rear, which is a good clue as to their former use. I personally enjoy nothing more than to look at these old buildings and try to imagine how they once looked. Try standing in Blundell's furnishing shop sometime and imagine how it must have once been. Where, for example, was the entrance? Why does the adjoining shop have such ornate pillars outside? Could this have once been the hotel's entrance?

A Street of Inns

In his book *Sittingbourne, and the Names of Lands and Houses in or near it. Their Origin and History*, published in 1879, W.A. Scott Robertson takes the reader on a virtual walk along our High Street, pointing out where some of these inns once were. He described Sittingbourne as being a street of inns during the reign of Queen Elizabeth I, a description that's so very true. He begins his walk at the Bull, an inn of long standing, by the entrance to what is now Roman Square. Next door, to the west, was the Horn, an early owner being John Norden in 1562. By 1820 it had become a private house belonging to Edward Brenchley and occupied by William Castle, a

One of Sittingbourne's old coaching inns, the George, that dates back to about 1685, in 2002. *(Sketch by David Colthup)*

surgeon. There was another inn squeezed in between the Bull and the Horn, but that was absorbed into the premises of the Bull at an unknown date. Beyond the Horn lay two more inns, the Saracen's Head and the Gun. Both date back to at least 1562. After ceasing to be an inn the Saracen's Head became a private house, while the Gun became the workhouse. By 1752 it was again an inn, this time called the Globe, but it was not to last for long as it soon reverted to being the workhouse. Eventually, when larger premises were found for the workhouse, the old inn became a coachmaker's workshop.

Another long-gone inn was the Hart's Horn that once stood near the junction of Ufton Lane and West Street, not to be confused with the site once occupied by the Volunteer, which is slightly further up the hill. Back in the High Street, Scott Robertson points out the location of another long-gone ancient inn, the Six Bells, which once stood between Berry Street and the entrance of the Forum Shopping Centre. Back in 1630 it had been known as the Kings Head, and from 1562 to 1574 was owned by John Norden who also owned the Horn. Soon after 1752 it became a private house, part of which became the workhouse at one stage.

Between this former inn and the Red Lion there had once been a forge, but during the reign of George I it had been an inn, the Black Boy. Mention has already been made of the Red Lion, but close by to the east before you came to the Rose was the Boatswain's Call, adjacent to which was the Chequer, which ceased as an inn some time prior to 1769. Following several changes in ownership, its eastern portion was turned into the Rose taproom, now occupied by a Wimpy bar. Beyond the Rose once stood the Swan. Next door to what is now Bateman's opticians, is a pet and garden shop that was once the Three Post Boys inn. After the church was the Bird in Hand inn in 1731, followed by the Fauken (Falcon?), an inn whose name in 1650 had been the Adam and Eve. The Fauken was built in 1562, but by 1769 had been extensively rebuilt as three separate houses. Its former names were completely forgotten.

Opposite St Michael's church, from where Sittingbourne developed, once stood the Angel Inn, which, by 1650, had reverted to being a private house, but it was demolished in 1735. Close by was the Portobello, popularly known as the Beggars Opera, but that too seems to have ceased trading by 1650. Next is the George, which has already been mentioned.

From this brief description you can indeed see that at various times there were many inns and hostelries scattered along the length of the High Street. There was a huge demand for them but no doubt many failed simply because they were too small to meet the demand. They could not compete with the larger establishments like the Red Lion, the George and the Rose.

SIX

Brickmaking and
Cement Manufacture

A s the trade generated by passing travellers and stagecoaches began to wane
following the invention of the steam engine, the future started to look bleak
for Sittingbourne. However, the repeal of the Brick Tax in 1850 brought
indirectly a new trade to the town upon which its fortunes were to grow. As the new
railway network expanded, it seemed to have an inexhaustible demand for bricks with a
high tensile strength for the many stations, tunnels and bridges along its routes. Many
of the villages around London began to grow at the end of the Napoleonic wars and
slowly became part of the metropolis. New buildings like the Law Courts, Tower
Bridge, Kings Cross station, Westminster Cathedral and Buckingham Palace started to
emerge. Their size required an especially strong brick and the Kentish Stock brick was
ideal. Sittingbourne quickly became the leading supplier of these bricks, and its
brickfields and cement manufacturing works became one of the largest industrial
complexes in southern England.

It was not a new skill but it did mark the start of a new way of making bricks.
Brickmaking, like pottery, is one of the oldest skills in the world. Traditional Kent bricks
date to Roman times and were red in colour, but they were flatter, looking more like
thick tiles than conventional bricks. Examples can be seen in the walls of the churches at
Milton, Teynham and Lower Halstow. After the Romans left few bricks were made in
Britain until the fifteenth century when it became fashionable for buildings to be
constructed partly or entirely of them. They were widely used for the façades of many of
our older, distinguished buildings. It marked the change from the earlier wattle and
daub huts to more substantially built buildings. Wherever towns or villages were situated
and brick-earth was available, there was sure to be a brickfield nearby. To begin with,
suitable clay was found around London itself, but as the deposits became worked out
and the land was needed to build upon, builders had to look further afield.

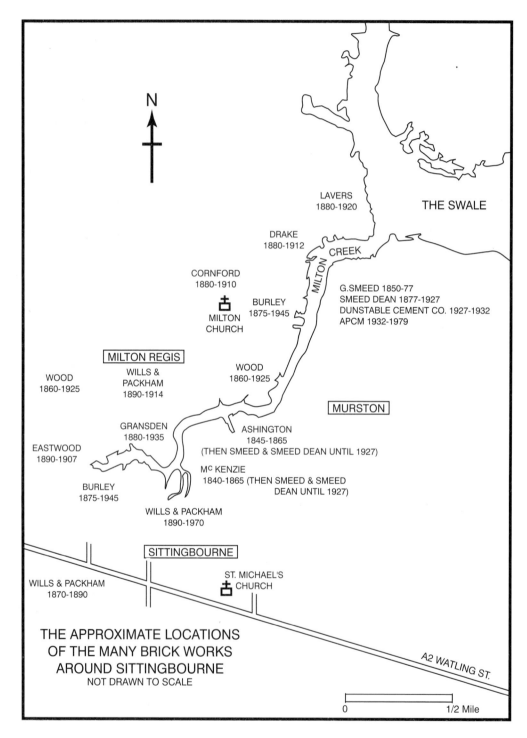

N

THE SWALE

LAVERS
1880-1920

DRAKE
1880-1912

MILTON CREEK

CORNFORD
1880-1910

BURLEY
1875-1945

MILTON
CHURCH

G.SMEED 1850-77
SMEED DEAN 1877-1927
DUNSTABLE CEMENT CO. 1927-1932
APCM 1932-1979

MILTON REGIS

WILLS &
PACKHAM
1890-1914

WOOD
1860-1925

WOOD
1860-1925

MURSTON

GRANSDEN
1880-1935

ASHINGTON
1845-1865
(THEN SMEED & SMEED DEAN UNTIL 1927)

EASTWOOD
1890-1907

Mᶜ KENZIE
1840-1865 (THEN SMEED & SMEED
DEAN UNTIL 1927)

BURLEY
1875-1945

WILLS & PACKHAM
1890-1970

SITTINGBOURNE

ST. MICHAEL'S
CHURCH

WILLS & PACKHAM
1870-1890

THE APPROXIMATE LOCATIONS
OF THE MANY BRICK WORKS
AROUND SITTINGBOURNE
NOT DRAWN TO SCALE

A2 WATLING ST.

0   1/2 Mile

The brick works around Sittingbourne. *(J. Clancy)*

The Discovery of the Stock Brick

The breakthrough in making harder, more durable, yellow stock bricks came in the 1740s when it was found that by mixing the brick-earth with ashes and chalk, a different sort of brick could be obtained. Whether this came about by accident or as a result of experimentation is not known. In his book *Stock Bricks of Swale* Sydney Twist, a former brickmaker and authority on the history of brickmaking, states he has never found the origins of the stock brick, who discovered it and where, but feels sure it had to be in or near Sittingbourne.

Previously bricks had been made of pure brick-earth and were baked in a kiln, fired with wood, coal or coke. The colour of the brick was determined by the amount of iron in the brick-earth. By mixing the brick-earth with ashes and chalk, the brick cooked from within as well and turned yellow. These new stock bricks were cheaper to make. Much of the cost involved in making bricks was in the price of the fuel used to bake them.

But the process was not quite as simple as it first looks. It must have taken a long time to work out the correct proportions of the ingredients, after which the burning rate had to be worked out by varying the proportions of materials and the way in which the bricks were stacked in the kiln. Eventually the technique was mastered and production began in earnest.

The brickmaking boom had begun, and many houses were built throughout this area in the seventeenth and eighteenth centuries using this new type of brick, including the former Rose inn in Sittingbourne High Street where Woolworths now is. Brickmaking had earlier been an industry too small to warrant a mention in any history book about the area, but from 1830 until 1870 it was the major local industry, employing over 50 per cent of our workforce. By the second half of the nineteenth century brickmaking had become a labour-intensive industry, and at the height of its production over 6,000 people were employed. A report in 1848 stated that our annual output of bricks was 30 million. By 1880 Smeed Dean alone was producing nearly 50 million bricks a year.

Geographically and geologically, Sittingbourne is well placed for being a major producer of bricks, and as was found later had an added bonus, the Creek, for transporting them. To carry bricks and cement to London, hundreds of sailing barges were built on the Creek and a new lifestyle evolved. This is looked at in chapter 8.

The best quality brick-earth contains windblown clay with appreciable amounts of sand and silt. A belt of this special clay runs from east to west from Rainham to Faversham, stretching back from the marshes in the north to about 200 ft south of the main road. Beyond that the land is very chalky. The third ingredient required for making stock bricks is ash, which was imported from major cities like London. A system evolved whereby barges took bricks to London and rather than return empty brought back the capital's ashes and rubbish. This was then used to make more bricks, so it could be said that London is largely built of its own rubbish.

It was a dangerous cargo to carry, as there was the ever-present danger of spontaneous combustion and carbon dioxide fumes given off by the coke. The barges were made of wood and if the cargo caught fire the crews stood little chance of saving their vessel. When this lethal cargo arrived in Sittingbourne it was dumped on what became known as the Dung Wharf and left to rot down in huge mounds for a year or more. After the vegetable matter had rotted down, women, children and old men, who were incapable of working in the brickfields for whatever reason, sorted the remainder. The fine ash left after much sieving was then mixed with the brick-earth and the coke was used to fire the kilns and clamps. Anything of value, such as jewellery, had to be handed to the moulders as their perks, and anything left that was usable was seized by the poorer brickfield workers who often lived in makeshift huts furnished with their finds.

The Early Brickfields

Some of the early brickfields were operated by the landowners using their existing workers, but most were worked by a master brickmaker who would lease a plot of land containing brick-earth from a farmer and pay him by the cubic foot for the material excavated. When the field had been worked out the topsoil was replaced so that the field could be recultivated within a short time. The only evidence left that the field had once been a brickfield was that it was lower than the adjoining ones. Unlike many other industries of the time that extracted raw materials from the earth, such as coal mining and gravel works, the landscape was not dramatically or permanently affected. At first agricultural workers from the owner's farm and itinerant workers enticed by the prospect of well-paid seasonal work formed the main workforce. Later, as the industry stabilised and started to grow with fixed sites, the job of brickie evolved for men who were prepared to work hard, accept piecework rates and take a keen interest in their job. Equipment needed to make bricks was minimal – a horse-driven pugmill, a bench on which to make the bricks, straw to cover the drying bricks for protection against rain or frost, some poles to hold down the straw and a kiln in which to bake the bricks.

Until 1865–70 there were no brickfields as such. Clay was dug out where it was found, washed in backs for eighteen months or more and then formed into kerfs, level piles about 3 ft high and 20 ft square. Upon this was placed 10 per cent of chalk by bulk and 25 per cent of finely screed rough stuff (ash and clinker). This heap was turned and mixed by hand between September and March ready for brickmaking in the spring and summer. When a new site for extracting brick-earth was being considered the company's directors would go to the field with their chemist, who would extract a

A type of field found in many parts of Swale, showing how after the extraction of brick-earth the land level becomes significantly lower. *(M. Clancy)*

soil sample with an auger. He would take a section of soil from the core, chew it for a while, then spit it out and declare whether it was suitable or not. Whether or not this is regarded as high science, he was rarely wrong. He couldn't be; his job and reputation depended upon it.

Digging for brick-earth was dangerous work, and in February 1859 a man was killed at Mr Huggens's brickfield. He had been digging out the clay, and after digging downwards, began to cut into the side of the hole, leaving a shelf of topsoil jutting out over him. Unfortunately it collapsed and fell on him, crushing him to death.

Child Labour

Until the passing of the Compulsory School Acts of 1872 many women and children worked in the brickfields, principally carrying clay from the mill to the moulder's table and loading the finished bricks on to barrows. The women sometimes did this, but were more often employed on 'flatting', or cutting, and rough-shaping lumps of clay with which the moulder could then make bricks.

It was common practice in the eighteenth and nineteenth centuries to employ women and children, and brickmaking was no exception. Often the moulders, as team leaders, would employ their own wife and children during the summer months when casual labour was scarce. This practice continued up until 1870 when one Act of Parliament made full-time schooling for children up to the age of ten compulsory, while another regulated the employment of children in the brickfields. A boy of ten could therefore work part time in the brickfields and when he reached the age of twelve or thirteen, leave school to take up full time employment. This continued until 1910 when half-time employment was stopped. Children could still leave school at the age of twelve or over if they had reached a required standard of education.

It was hard work, and in the early days there was no shelter to work beneath if the weather was wet. If the weather was particularly hot workers would start work at 3 or 4 a.m. and work until 10 a.m. They rested during the heat of the day and recommenced at about 3 or 4 p.m., working through until the evening.

One of the first local brickfields was established in 1835 by a Milton businessman by the name of Muggleton. It was near Adelaide Dock, where a stream flowed into the Creek and had for centuries been a small harbour. The brickfield stretched back from the waterfront to the Golden Ball orchard. Mr Muggleton built half a dozen brick huts for his workers about 100 yards away on the town side of the dock. Later he built another six nearer to the road, which in 1920 were used as a tile works. Near the dock he built stables and a single-storey brick building with two stone fodder lofts at one end and a horse keeper's house at the other. This was later used as a general store and a workshop where sieves and screens were made and repaired. By 1928 it had become a wheelwright's shop, but in 1929 burned down.

Mr Muggleton was not a brickmaker by trade, and some of his workers were brought in from Essex. They were described in reports of the time as being good brickmakers, even though rough and tough. In his history book of Murston, Sydney Twist, himself a former brickmaker, tells how his great-grandfather, a former Royal Marine Colour Sergeant of thirty years, became foreman of such a brickfield after being demobbed. He knew nothing about bricks but he certainly knew how to manage men. Soon after an outbreak of cholera in the Adelaide Dock area in 1849, the brickfield was taken over by George Smeed, and right up to the end of the brickmaking era the wharf on the south side of Adelaide Dock was always known as Muggleton's Wharf.

Another early brickmaker was Mr McKenzie who had a site between Adelaide Dock and Bayford Farm, Moat Road. It was started between 1840 and 1845. McKenzie also built brick huts for his workers on the opposite side of Moat Road to his stables. Nearby was a chalk pit, which supplied all the Murston brickfields until Smeed Dean started the Highsted pit in the 1890s. George Smeed bought the brickfield in 1865.

The third early Murston brickfield, started sometime between 1843 and 1845, was owned by Mr Ashington and lay between the new church and Adelaide Dock. He built

Adelaide Dock, in the former heartland of industrial Murston, in its heyday in the 1920s. The barge in the foreground is being loaded with bricks. The loaders' barrows are wheeled up a staging across the barge's decks to be stacked in the hold. *(Lafarge Cement)*

From once being an important wharf, Adelaide Dock is now slowly being filled in to form a lorry park. *(M. Clancy)*

Clamp brickmaking at Upper Field in 1928. Note the scintled bricks and layers of coke breeze. *(Lafarge Cement)*

eight huts for his workers, the bricks for which were all stamped with the letter O, signifying they had been made by Owen of Faversham. These cottages were demolished in 1937. Mr Ashington made mostly traditional red bricks, and when the foremen's houses opposite the church were demolished soon after 1971, Sydney Twist remembers finding red bricks stamped with the letter A for Ashington on the site. Like the others, this field was acquired by George Smeed in 1865.

By the middle of the nineteenth century the brickmaking boom was well established with brickfields laid out as are generally known today, operating all over Swale and changing the look of some areas completely. The greatest development was in an area stretching from Murston, to the north-east of Sittingbourne, along the eastern banks of the Creek, and to the east and west of Sittingbourne. This was where the Smeed Dean partnership, the firm at the heart of the expanding industry, was centred. There were other brickfields, large and small, throughout Milton as well.

Smeed Dean

The founder of this partnership, George Smeed, was one of the industrial stalwarts of the nineteenth century, a man with vision and a flair for organisation, and was said to be a man of strong habits – and even stronger language. With so many business connections at his fingertips he quickly earned the nickname George Bargebrick Esq. He was the last to start brickmaking in Murston, and after buying out all the other established fields, created the largest stock brick works in the district as well as the industrial village of Lower Murston.

Born of a fishing family at Elmley in 1812, George Smeed was described as being a man of humble origins who was ill-educated and had a background as a street-hawker, smuggler, jailbird and a man deeply into many businesses, one of which was the gas works at Crown Quay Lane. Considerable profits could be made from investing in gas works, and after Milton's had been established Smeed invited some London financiers down to explain how to subscribe to an issue. Initially he wanted to supply coal to the gas works, but after listening to their explanation Smeed asked the financiers whether there was any limit to the number of shares a subscriber could buy. When told there was not, he told the financiers he would buy the entire subscription. And so George Smeed became the proprietor of Sittingbourne's gas works.

His early business interests were more connected with coal than bricks – in the census returns of 1841 he describes himself as a coal merchant. He owned colliers, wharves, a shipyard and a sail loft, but the turning point came when he acquired a smallholding in Sittingbourne, which included a small brickworks. After that he never looked back and went on to become a justice of the peace, a well-respected citizen and a gentleman with a large mansion at Gore Court. His name became a byword in brickmaking. His was one of the great success stories of the nineteenth-century industrial age.

George Smeed invested a small legacy in land, and having made a profit from it invested in more land, buying out the leases of other small local brickmakers until his Murston works was the largest in the world. He began brickmaking in 1846 on the south-east side of Church Road, where he built two blocks of four brick huts for his workers. They were demolished at the turn of the twentieth century, but by then he had started to expand in a big way. These huts were of a standard design in the 1830s and 1840s with two rooms, each being 9 or 10 ft square with a tiny 6 ft square kitchen attached. By the 1850s, with increased output and higher earnings, the workers were able to afford a better standard of living and two-storey tied cottages of four or six rooms were built for them.

George Smeed next built eight houses in Gas Road, opposite the old church, the end one of which was a shop and post office but later converted to a private house. In

An outing of the Smeed Dean brickies in 1913, in an open top Straker & Squire omnibus, departing from what is probably the old Swan Inn at Greenstreet before the new pub was built. *(Lafarge Cement)*

Church Road he built a terrace of ten houses, the first of which was a shop with a bakehouse at the rear. This was where the post office relocated to and together with the shop remained until demolished in 1965. A third house had the downstairs rooms knocked into one and was the school until 1868, after which it became the Murston Social Club.

More and more houses were built in Church Road and Gas Road, and in 1882 Smeed demolished his Murston Manor to build a further eight houses. In 1859 he built the Brickmakers Arms public house, and when applying for a licence told the magistrates that the public house was needed not only for his brickfield and gas works employees, but also for the crews of the sixty barges that used his wharf, not that all of these were his, but at the time he did have a sizeable fleet, having acquired the shipyard at the bottom of Stable Road. What a lively mixture of drinkers there must have been in the Brickmakers Arms at that time.

Joining George Smeed in 1865 was John Andrews, an experienced brickmaker who knew all about stock brickmaking. He was appointed brickfield foreman, and in 1875 was promoted to director and general manager of the works, a position he held for thirty years. He was a stern disciplinarian and a good organiser of the manual side of the business, and later both he and his son, George, who was managing director for over twenty years, dominated both the works and the village. John Andrews, George Smeed and his son-in-law, George Hambrook Dean, were responsible for shaping the company and placing it in a strong position to survive the brick industry's depressed years from the 1880s to the start of the First World War.

George Smeed built his first washmill to separate the stone and coarse sand from the clay in about 1865; it was sited behind the houses opposite the old church. Very soon they were springing up all over Murston as George Smeed opened more and more brickworks. Washmills were not a new invention, having been used in the pottery industry for a hundred years or more. To begin with horses drove the washmills, but soon they were converted to steam power.

Washmills fixed the brickfields to one site thus creating brickworks rather than brickfields. The layout of each site was roughly the same in design with a row of washbacks, against which were sheds in rows about 100 ft apart through each of which ran a drive shaft powering a pug mill. The engine shed was usually in the middle. Radiating out from the sheds at right angles were rows of drying hacks 150 ft long. By 1870–5 the horse mill had been replaced in most brickworks by a power-driven pugmill.

Brickmakers worked in teams of six consisting of three men, one youth and two boys. Each had a specific job to do. The 'temperer' loaded the clay into the pug mill, adding water if the clay was too stiff or lime if too soft. The 'flatty' then cut off a lump of clay weighing about 8½lb, as it came from the mill and held it ready for the 'moulder', who was the team leader. The moulder then made the bricks by placing the clay on a frame called a page, which weighed about 3lb. It had to be washed and scraped every five minutes or so, adding to the time taken to make the brick. The next member of the team, the 'barrow loader', would take the bricks and stack them on the barrow, ready for the 'pushie' to wheel out to the drying area, or hack, where the 'offbearer', the team's number two, would transfer the bricks to the drying boards. When dry, the bricks were taken by the 'crowders' and built into clamp kilns by the 'moulder setter' who was responsible for burning the bricks. The final process was when the clamps were dismantled and the bricks graded by 'sorters'.

Brickmakers were paid at piecework rates, which the team leader, the moulder, fixed with the owner or brickmaster. In the early days, when agricultural workers were used, they knew nothing about the price for the job and would work flat out for 20 or 25s a week, nearly twice their farm wages, ignorant that by their efforts they had earned the rest of the team probably twice as much.

The average moulder could make 30 barrowloads of bricks per hour. A barrow held 30 bricks so this amounted to 900 bricks per hour. In the course of a typical ten-hour day one team's output would be nearly 10,000 bricks. A wet brick weighed about 6lb. By the 1870s the different jobs had been graded and a foreman controlled the labour.

The gang leaders would always draw the wages for the job and share them out among the gang, who would all know the price for the job and what their share would be.

Brickmaking was a seasonal job, but in the winter months work digging clay could usually be found for the moulder and sometimes the temperer. The youths and boys would often screen the roughstuff or unload the sand barges, work in the flint pits or load flints into the barges. Flint stones were a byproduct of chalk excavation and were used in road making. This was a time when there was no dole, so if you didn't work you starved: anything was better than nothing.

Record-Breaking Brickmakers

Brickmaking, although a harsh and hard life, was an honoured profession with many sons proudly following in their father's footsteps. In a newspaper report of October 1935 it was reported that a team of Murston brickmakers had made 1 million bricks in a twenty-seven-week season. Such quantities were often produced before the First World War but not after. This was because by the 1930s workers were working twelve hours a week less than before the war, and as a competitive market demanded a better-made brick, production was slower, so to exceed 1 million bricks per season was a difficult goal to achieve.

The record was achieved by two gangs of three men and three boys, employed by Associated Portland Cement Ltd. In each team two men took it in turn to make bricks for an hour at the time. While one was making, another set the bricks to dry. To complete the million in the allotted time, they had to average 900 per hour, or four seconds per brick. The 1935 record-breaking team consisted of Mr A. Nash, Mr H. Nash and Mr A. Hopkins. The Nash brothers had made bricks since they were boys and had followed their father into the business. The other team consisted of brothers P. Fletcher and C. Fletcher, and Mr G. Newman. Like the Nashes the Fletchers had also been lifelong brickmakers and had followed their father and grandfather into the business.

Until the twentieth century horses played a great part in most people's lives. Smeed Dean bred a lot of their own for work in the brickfields powering the pugmills. Up to 1878 each of Murston's brickworks had their own individual stables, but then George Smeed built a new central stable block, cart shed and paddock on the corner of the Golden Ball orchard with accommodation for fifty horses. When the work was completed he gave his workmen a supper in the new stable block. This building was in use up to the outbreak of the Second World War, and in 1960 was converted into APCM's social club.

George Smeed was said to be a great believer in feudalism and believed in sharing pleasure with his workers. No matter how bad the conditions under which they

George Smeed's stumpy barge *Alfred* discharging at Putney. *Alfred* is an old-fashioned barge, built at Bankside in 1847, with a 'Roman-nosed' bow. Note the wooden stayfall blocks. *(Lafarge Cement)*

laboured, the workers greatly respected him. It was typical of the man that whenever a new vessel was launched the shipyard workers would be invited to Gore Court for a party followed by a cricket match and a late evening supper. Alcoholic drinks were freely served, which was frowned upon by other employers in the town who celebrated their launches with 'temperance teas' by way of a protest. Despite Smeed having a liberal attitude towards his workers, he neither encouraged nor discouraged morality, and would not allow alcohol to be sold on Sundays or his workers to work on that day.

Industrial Unrest

Smeed never had any trouble with his workers apart from an isolated incident with his shipwrights in the 1860s over a minor matter, which was soon settled. Trade unionism was starting to grow, but there is no evidence of trade-union membership among Smeed's workers until 1890. Following a strike in 1889 London dockers got an increase in their pay. Their success led to the formation of the Society for the Protection of Bargemen and Watermen (see chapter 8). As the bargemen were unhappy with their pay structure, they also came out on strike. The effect it had upon the local community was devastating. The brickworks owners had no alternative but to lock out their workers, as they could not afford to stockpile the bricks.

By the end of the second week the strike and lock-out had extended right along the Kent coast. Sittingbourne was at the centre of the dispute and in March 1889, over 5,000 brickies from Faversham, led by a brass band, marched in procession to Sittingbourne with colleagues from Conyer, Murston, Sittingbourne and Milton to attend a meeting addressed by the vice-president of the Bargemen's Society, Mr Tookey, a representative of the London Dock, Wharf and General Labourers Union, Mr W. Nicholls and Mr Cunningham-Gibson MP. It was an unbelievable demonstration of solidarity by brickies who had traditionally always been at odds with the bargemen. Three days later another march of 3,000 workers processed through the town carrying banners with slogans like 'Stick like Bricks'. Solidarity was the order of the day and at this meeting it was agreed that the bargemen would accept arbitration.

In Sittingbourne a relief committee was quickly organised and soup kitchens set up, although the workers were reluctant to accept help, seeing it as poor-law relief. The stigma attached to this by decent, honest working people at the time was widely recognised. The relief committee was so over-enthusiastic that after a couple of weeks they had overspent their funds and were forced to withdraw their help. With no reconciliation in sight by April, economic developments in another part of the country started to affect the dispute. As brickmaking started to develop in Peterborough, using rail transport to London, it gave real cause for concern that important markets for Sittingbourne stock bricks would be lost.

Despite the brickworks' owners drawing up a new list of suggested payments for carrying freight, claiming they represented a 10 per cent increase on the old rates, the bargemen firmly rejected it. An attempt was made to break the strike when two of Wills and Packham's barges sailed down the Creek, but they and some of the Smeed Dean barges were prevented from leaving by other vessels forming a barrier. Aboard one of the blocking barges was Mr Cole, the portreeve of Milton, who defiantly read from the town's charter that he had the right to close the Creek. Despite this abuse of the royal charter to further the cause of the strikers, Mr Cole was later re-elected. Finally, at the end of April 1889, the strike was called off and the bargemen accepted new freight rates drawn up by the owners and the brickmakers were allowed back to work again.

The industry grew rapidly in the nineteenth century and declined just as rapidly in the early part of the twentieth. It continued to dominate the local economy during the final decade of the nineteenth century with nearly 45 per cent of Sittingbourne's population working in either the brickmaking or cement-manufacturing industries. By the end of the nineteenth century things had changed dramatically. The new housing trusts and councils building in London's suburbs were no longer interested in the qualities of the stock brick; they wanted cheaper bricks, a market quickly filled by imports from Belgium. The Kentish stock brick was priced out of the market. But despite this the stock brick remains the best brick for house building.

In the face of falling demand and increased competition the price of stock bricks fell, resulting, in 1906, in a cut in brickmakers' pay. Local brickworks owners also faced increased costs when the Milton Creek Conservancy Board introduced a levy on goods entering and leaving the Creek. Instead of helping to keep the Creek open, as had been the original purpose of the Conservancy Board, it had the completely opposite effect and helped to contribute to its demise as a major waterway. With this additional financial burden many of the smaller firms went out of business. The amount of traffic using the Creek declined, it began to silt up and eventually became unnavigable.

However, none of this seriously affected the Smeed Dean partnership with its diverse business interests, each helping the other to survive. In 1906 it opened a new red brick plant with a Monarch brick-moulding machine. It was capable of making 5 million bricks per year. The firm also installed a continuous kiln, attached to which were drying and tempering rooms where the bricks could be dried using ducted hot air, so brickmaking could now be carried out all year round. A second plant opened in 1911, the year when brickworks owners faced strikes, not only from their own men, but also from the bargemen who had been badly hit by a slump in the brick trade during the first decade of the new century. They were on a slippery slope, and by the 1930s Smeed Dean, who had the largest fleet of barges, sold it, marking the end of an occupation that had played an important part in the area's economy.

A Royal Visit

In 1921 the Duke of York, later George VI, visited Swale, and Smeed Dean published a brochure about the company. In it they quoted its average annual output to be in excess of 52 million bricks per year. They proudly claimed to be the oldest and largest manufacturer of stock bricks in the country. Their bricks, each stamped with the initials SD, had been used in the construction of many important buildings including Buckingham Palace, the Great Exhibition at Crystal Palace in 1851, the Law Courts,

Tower Bridge, Kings Cross station, Westminster cathedral, the London docks and many public buildings, offices and homes. The SD stamped on each brick was, of course, the company's initials, but many said it also stood for 'Strength and Durability'.

By then Smeed Dean was also manufacturing cement and the brochure quoted output of 1,500 tons per week. As flint was extracted from the chalk before the process began, it was put to good use in road building and this branch of the Smeed Dean empire employed 1,208 men, women and boys. Until the early 1920s most of the company's bricks, cement and flints were dispatched by waterborne transport, as Smeed Dean had by this time about 100 barges.

The End of an Era

George Smeed died in May 1881 at the age of sixty-nine and in his will left a sum of money for bread and coal to be distributed to the elderly of Murston at Christmas. His obituary claimed that 'He may almost be said to have made Sittingbourne what it is.' Smeed was responsible for changing the character of the town from one whose economy was based on agriculture to one of the most concentrated industrial complexes outside the Midlands or the North of England. With kiln and clamp fires raging day and night throughout the summer months, it must have been akin to the foundry fires of Coalbrookdale in Shropshire. Each successive tide brought in fleets of barges laden with London's rubbish, which was dumped in huge mounds on the bank of the Creek where it awaited rotting down and sorting. The stench must have been overpowering.

Smeed's son-in-law, George Hambrook Dean, chairman of the Smeed Dean Co. from 1875, died in 1924 aged ninety-one. He had been a good businessman and over the years had a great influence on the progress of the company. He was also one of the most prominent farmers in the district.

In 1926 the company was sold to the newly formed Dunstable Cement Co., which in 1928 merged with others to form the Red Triangle Combine. The company was acquired by the APCM group in November 1931.

While much of the local brickmaking industry was centred in Murston, there were brickworks in other parts of the district. John Huggens started one of the first brickworks in Fairmeadow, Crown Quay Lane, in the early 1830s. It was managed by Richard Orgles. There was a large double-fronted house adjoining the field, built either for himself or for his foreman. A tablet built into the front of the house was dated 1835, so this makes the brickworks one of the first stock brickfields in this area. That house, like the brickworks site, has long disappeared beneath modern development. John Huggens had a barge named after him, built in 1866, so we can assume he still had the brickworks then. The works was taken over by Wills and Packham in about

Chilton manor house was once the home of brickmaker Chas Burley. *(M. Clancy)*

1870. They also had a small field at what is now the junction of Crown Quay Lane and St Michael's Road. The washbacks were adjacent to the back gardens of some houses further away in East Street. In its later stages the brickworks stretched from Crown Quay Lane to Princes Street and down to the Creek. A public footpath bounded its southern boundary, running between it and the railway line. As a small boy I can well recall walking along that trackway which ran from New Road to Murston Road. Today a major road has been built on it to take vehicles into the business park that now stands on the site of the brickworks which closed in about 1970.

Adjoining the Wills and Packham field was another, run by Chas Burley, which operated from 1875 to 1945. He had a larger field near Milton church, which similarly closed in 1945 after being hit by a flying bomb, or doodlebug, towards the end of the Second World War. At that time I lived nearby in Grovehurst Road and can still recall the night the flying bomb was downed by a Spitfire. Opposite Wills and Packham's wharf, between Milton's workhouse and the Creek, was Gransden's brickfield, which began manufacturing bricks in 1880 and continued to do so until 1935.

Mr Wood had a small brickfield in Milton, lying between those of Gransden and Burley, which operated between 1860 and 1925; their second site was in Staplehurst Road. A Mr Cornford ran the brickfield to the west of Burley's field behind Milton church between 1880 and 1910. It was a small field with just three horse mills and was the last field locally to use them. Other smaller fields included those of Lavers

(1880–1920) and Drake (1880–1912), both of which were at Kemsley near the mouth of the Creek, and Eastwoods to the west of Sittingbourne (1890–1907).

Despite being principally a town, Sittingbourne itself was not without its own brickfields. One of its earliest was to the south of the main road in the vicinity of what is now Valenciennes Road. It was the first to be operated by Wills and Packham when they came to Sittingbourne from Rainham in about 1870. It was a small site and closed down in about 1890. Another lay close by at this time in the vicinity of the junction of Ufton Lane and West Street and was owned by a Mr Cremer who later sold it to Burley's.

Following production changes developed elsewhere there was a large reduction in the workforce when increased mechanisation was introduced. In 1926 the Lower Field at Murston was rebuilt with an automatic brick plant. A new American 'Auto-brik' machine was installed, which was said to be the fastest brickmaking plant in the country, producing 10,000 bricks per hour. It replaced the need for eleven hand-making gangs. Another new innovation came in 1929 with a 560-ft-long tunnel kiln, through which cars loaded with bricks ran on a railway track. As one car was loaded and pushed in with a ram, the last car was pushed out of the other end.

The brickworks was closed down for most of the Second World War but restarted in May 1946 when the tunnel kiln was relit. It then burned continuously until September 1979, firing over 1,000 million bricks. The Monarch berths set up in 1906 were closed down in 1965, and as the old auto-plant closed a new one opened where five men could produce the same number of bricks that it would have taken seventy-eight to make in the days of hand-production. The raw materials were by now being imported from outside the area by lorry. Even though the roughstuff was no longer being brought in, there was still a plentiful supply that had been brought in 100 years before. In all the time stock bricks had been made, no substitute for the ash and clinker content was ever found. As more and more houses acquired central heating and open coal fires became a thing of the past, there was little roughstuff available to provide the means for cheap burning.

Clamp burning was reintroduced in 1979, with the clamps being built in much the same way as they had been in the nineteenth century, only now they were fired by natural gas instead of bundles of wood – but sorting was still done by hand. The Murston works remained the only brickworks owned by APCM until they bought up the brickmaking firm Ottley Bricks, a name they kept and used for all their brickworks including Murston. Despite this, the finished bricks continued to be stamped with the initials SD.

Smeed Dean was not the only brickmaker to continue into the twentieth century. In 1950 Wills and Packham celebrated with a team who had made 1 million bricks during the season, and ten years later finally pensioned off the 'Bellfield Thunderer', a steam-driven engine that drove an earth-washing machine. It had been in operation for 100 years. Wills and Packham closed in 1969 with the loss of fifty jobs.

Serving as a poignant reminder of the area's once thriving barge industry is this building at Crown Quay, which is thought to be the last of the old quayside warehouses. *(M. Clancy)*

While much is attributed to George Smeed, it should be remembered that Mr Daniel Wills, one half of Wills and Packham, also made a significant contribution to the town. Following an accident in his brickworks he organised an appeal in 1898 that raised sufficient money to buy Sittingbourne's first ambulance. Mrs G.H. Dean donated a second ambulance in 1912, the first motor ambulance in Kent and claimed to be the best in England.

After such a glorious, even if short-lived, past brickmaking is now a negligible contributor to Swale's economy.

Cement Manufacturing

Just as George Smeed had played a pivotal role in Sittingbourne's brickmaking industry, so he did in two other local allied industries: the manufacture of cement and barge building. There were two important landmarks in the development of the cement industry in this area. The first was during the early part of the nineteenth century following the expiration of Joseph Parker's Roman cement patent in 1810. Parker's method was to use septaria stone, found in clay on the banks of the Swale. After being

An aerial view of the Smeed Dean works at Murston, 1920. In the bottom left-hand corner is Adelaide Dock. To the right of the gasometer, through the smoke, is Murston's old church. *(Aerofilms)*

dug out, it was burnt in alternate layers with coal in a bottle kiln and after cooling, was crushed into a powder in horse mills.

Sam Shepherd of Faversham is credited as being the first local cement manufacturer to begin operations in 1812. He founded works that later became Hilton, Anderson and Brooks. Brothers Samuel and Charles Cleaver opened Sittingbourne's first cement mill at Bayford in the early 1820s. During a thunderstorm in 1860 the chimney was struck by lightning and the top 30 ft was lost. In 1866 there was another disaster when a fatal explosion in the engine house, with the Roman kilns on one side, and the grinding mills behind it, was destroyed. John Huggens also opened a cement works at Crown Quay in the 1830s, followed by another by George Baker.

In the 1850s George Smeed introduced Portland Cement from a mill by Adelaide Dock. Although this new manufacturing process was much the same as before, it was the ingredients that differed. Coal was replaced by gas coke, a much cheaper alternative following the development of Smeed's new gas works, and the septaria stone was replaced by a mixture of chalk and mud. The chalk was extracted from quarries on Smeed's land, firstly at East Hall, Murston, and later from Highsted, where the chalk was dug out by hand and after being washed was pumped through pipes to the Murston works. It was the best way to get the chalk transported noiselessly by day and night without the slightest interference to traffic or damage to the roads. The third ingredient, mud, was in plentiful supply, especially from the marshy islands known as the Lillies at the mouth of the Creek.

Although George Smeed had played a key role in the development of cement manufacture in this area, the Murston Cement Works did not retain his name for long. By 1869 he had leased it to Webster and Co., a company of which he was a partner. Two years later Webster and Co. formed a limited liability company called the Burham Brick, Lime and Cement Co. Ltd, of which George Smeed was a director until his death in 1881.

By the final decade of the nineteenth century there were a number of medium-sized firms manufacturing bricks, but they were all dominated by Smeed Dean with its interconnected businesses of cement manufacture, agriculture and barge building. As well as satisfying the local market, much of the Portland cement was sent abroad as well, but that changed with the dawning of the twentieth century. Other countries, such as the United States, started developing their own cement-making facilities and the export trade started to fall. The situation was further aggrieved when Belgium and Germany began exporting cement into Britain. It was of a poorer quality than Portland cement, but it was cheaper, and that appealed to some buyers. It was not only the local cement works that were to suffer, but also others elsewhere. Some closed down completely, while others amalgamated in 1900 to form the Associated Portland Cement Manufacturers, known more commonly as APCM.

Smeed Dean's Murston cement works, which had earlier been leased to the Burham Brick, Lime and Cement Co., remained independent until 1924. This was made possible because of the way the company was run and because the other parts of the business helped it survive. It was not often that the same firm manufactured bricks and cement. Furthermore, the situation was also greatly helped by the fact that Smeed Dean continued to use chamber kilns built with their own bricks, thus avoiding having to recoup the high capital outlay faced by other firms who had installed costly rotary kilns.

In the late 1920s Smeed Dean changed over to rotary kilns, but only after they had joined the remaining independent manufacturers to form the Red Triangle

The great chamber kilns built in 1900 at the south-east corner of the Murston Cement Works in 1921, with slurry pipes running along the top. In 1926–8 they were demolished and replaced with Smidth kilns. (Lafarge Cement)

Quarrying for flints at Highsted. *(Sittingbourne Heritage Museum)*

Group. These new kilns had to be fired by coal, not coke, which came by rail from a colliery near Canterbury. In 1931 the Red Triangle Group merged with APCM, which opened up a new quarry at Highsted using mechanical excavation rather than the old method of blasting. APCM brought in some of their workers from other works and made many Murston men redundant. When this news was announced Les Dawkins, one of the APCM workers, was in church awaiting the arrival of his bride-to-be. Instead, in strode George Andrews clutching a piece of paper telling Les his services were to be retained by the new company as shipping manager. Mr V.S. Beal was appointed as APCM's first general manager at Murston.

In the early 1970s cement manufacture in Murston came to an end. The decision to close down the Murston works was made on economic grounds. Murston was a small part of APCM's overall operation and announced they intended to centre their production at Northfleet. Despite a huge local outcry that over 200 employees would lose their jobs, APCM is reported as having said they were closing the works with the greatest regret, but at the same time wished to thank all the former employees for their loyal service over a period of many years. The following year the 230-ft chimney of the old APCM works was demolished, removing the final tangible reminder of what had once been an important industry. The site of the old brick and cement works has now been razed to the ground and an industrial estate built on it. Even Adelaide Dock, with all its historic connections, has been lost to modern developments. Nothing, it seems, is sacred any more. Photos and memories are all that remain of a once proud and industrious community.

SEVEN
Papermaking

As has been seen in previous chapters, the streams that once crossed the main road on their way to Milton Creek have played an important part in the overall development of the town. Sittingbourne itself grew from the settlement that once stood on the banks of the stream that flowed down Bell Road. The stream that rose in the vicinity of Borden Lane and Chalkwell Road supported the watermills and tanneries along its entire length, while the third, flowing down Ufton Lane, supplied water for the paper mill.

The busy crossroads of West Street, Ufton Lane and the end of the ring road, St Michael's Road, is now completely different to how it looked 100 years ago. Before the ring road was built in the 1970s it was partly a series of side roads and backstreets, and readers will doubtless remember that this end of the road was Cockleshell Walk. On entering the road from West Street the stream could clearly be seen on the right.

A hundred years ago or more Cockleshell Walk was known as Water Lane and it led into a 2-acre plot known as Borden Mead. In Elizabethan times there had been a large house here called Borden House which was demolished during the seventeenth century, but despite this the name remained with the site. Even though the land was in the manor of Bayford, the Earl of Chesterfield, the lord of Chilton Manor, owned it in 1721. In the eighteenth century it passed through the Harvey, Baldock and Morrison families, and by 1835 was owned by William Palfrey who built a cottage there. To the north of Borden Mead stood the paper mill.

Early Papermaking

Local parish registers of the eighteenth century record that there was a paper mill in Sittingbourne run by the Archer family. An inventory dated 1737 shows that Robert Archer had six pairs of moulds, one engine, three presses, four tons of hand rags and seventy reams of paper. It was clearly a different process to that used today, with pounded rags being used instead of wood pulp.

By 1752 the mill had passed into the hands of William Stevens, and in the early nineteenth century Edward Smith, who lived in Love Lane (later renamed Mill Street), Milton Regis. Some handmade paper later found in a solicitors' office bore the watermark of 'E. Smith 1820' with the Britannia double foolscap mark. According to the national census returns, in 1841 there were ten papermakers living in the same area as Smith who continued to make paper until 1850 when the mill fell into decline. The census return of 1851 shows only one papermaker living in Milton.

It is not known exactly why the mill went into decline, but one suggestion is that perhaps Smith had tried to move from making paper by hand to making it by Fourdrinier machines, which were difficult to operate without highly skilled operators. Another suggestion is that papermaking needs a considerable amount of water, and in 1858 a new road bridge was built across the head of the Creek, obstructing the mill's flow of water. Smith ordered his men to demolish the bridge. In the previous year Smith had lodged an objection to the East Kent Railway Bill that was going through Parliament on the grounds that if the line was built as proposed, it would render the mill useless for papermaking because of the smoke and dust from the railway. This is another indication that the paper was being made by hand, as the process requires a clean atmosphere. Whatever the reason, by 1861 there is no evidence of anyone making paper in Sittingbourne or Milton.

The Coming of Edward Lloyd

With the mill no longer in use, it came to the attention of Edward Lloyd, a papermaker with a small mill at Boxbridge on the River Lea to the north-east of London. Lloyd supplied the newsprint for his newspaper *Lloyd's Weekly London Newspaper*. He had purchased the Sittingbourne mill in 1863, and in August of that year it caught fire and was destroyed. It was not until 1866 that building work started on a new, much larger mill nearer to the railway line, which suggests that Lloyd was using a different method of production to Smith who had been so concerned with pollution from the railway. In the following year the shafts were ready to be erected, but it was expected that it would take a further two years to complete the building works. It was anticipated that the new mill's output would be 50 tons of paper per week compared with the 36 tons being made at the Boxbridge mill.

The business was very much a family-run concern and by 1871 Edward Lloyd and his wife Mareanne had moved to a house in Lloyd's Square close to the paper mill. He did not play an active part in public life, but despite this was made a member of London's Reform Club in recognition of services rendered to the Liberal Party. After he died in 1890, his eldest son Frank took over the business. In 1871 the business was still being run on a small scale with six paper-mill workers, one printer and five

An aerial view of Lloyd's paper mill, 1920. Many of the streets and houses surrounding the mill have now been demolished and the landscape today is vastly different. *(Aerofilms)*

labourers. Ten years later, however, it was starting to grow with eleven papermakers, a storekeeper, a nightwatchman, a gatekeeper, three stokers, two engine fitters and two engineers all being shown in the census returns.

In 1876 Edward Lloyd purchased the *Daily Chronicle* newspaper, formerly the *Clerkenwell News*, for which he had to have a new papermaking machine installed by G. & W. Bertram of Edinburgh. It was the largest machine at the time, capable of producing 1,300 sq ft of paper per minute. Management of the Sittingbourne mill was put in the hands of another of Edward Lloyd's sons, Frederick, and in 1882 the full papermaking process was transferred from London to Sittingbourne. In reporting this, the local newspaper mentioned that the mill was using 400 tons of coal and 80 tons of straw per week.

Fire broke out in the mill in 1883, destroying some three to four hundred reels of paper. With such a volatile and combustible product and materials, fire was a constant threat. By the 1860s, as rags were in short supply, it was found that straw and esparto grass from Spain and Algeria, where Lloyd held rights to huge areas of land, were a suitable substitute. Local seafaring brothers Isaiah and Ebenezer Shrubsall regularly shipped aboard Lloyd's schooner barge the *Emily Lloyd* on a 5,000-mile round trip for the grass.

Shovelling coal into boilers at Sittingbourne Mill. *(Bowater Paper Organisation Ltd)*

The mill was enlarged in 1884 and a new boiler house with eight steel boilers and a 110 ft chimney was built. By then the mill had three large papermaking machines in operation. Further improvements followed in 1888 with the addition of a powerful horizontal engine, two steam-driven travelling cranes and a new papermaking machine. The mill continued to increase its workforce, and by 1891 had over 140 employees.

Lloyds became a limited liability company in 1890 with capital of £250,000, and in 1892 formally opened a new mill within the substantial Sittingbourne complex. The architecture of the new mill was described as being in the Queen Anne style, and it soon accounted for about a third of the whole complex's 300 tons of paper produced each week. Newsprint was by now being exported to Australia and the west coast of Africa as well as being used by an ever-increasing home market.

Unlike the brickmaking and cement-manufacturing industries, which had faced production problems in the early twentieth century, the papermaking industry entered a period of growth, which was in no small way due to the earlier efforts of Edward Lloyd and his son Frank who were at the forefront of new developments in the industry. Having used straw and esparto grass for many years, Edward Lloyd turned to using wood pulp as his raw material and was one of the first papermakers to do so. For this he purchased a pulp mill in Norway.

Despite another fire in May 1900, by 1902 there were eleven papermaking machines on the Sittingbourne site, the largest being machine no. 11 that produced 550 ft of paper per minute. In the early years of the new century the price of paper had increased enormously, causing concern for some newspaper owners, but not Mr Pearson, who had purchased the *Daily Express* in 1900. Fortunately, upon acquiring the newspaper, he had entered into an agreement with Frank Lloyd, the only papermaker who would agree to supply him with the quantity of newsprint he required at any price. Lloyd not only supplied his competitors with newsprint, but also with anything else they wanted in a printing works from rotary machines to cotton waste. He seems to have had a policy of wide diversification while remaining in the overall field of papermaking, like other industrialists of the time.

Millworkers checking paper as it moves through machines. *(Bowater Paper Organisation Ltd)*

In continuing their practice of being at the forefront of new technological developments, two employees, Charles Martin, mill superintendent, and Mr Hutchinson, chief engineer, found that by tilting the wire table upon which the paper was made, the machine could produce good quality paper at much greater speeds. Mr Martin told the American manufacturers of the machine about his discovery and they modified some of their machines accordingly. The idea was later patented by a man named Eibel who started litigation against Lloyds for infringement. Frank Lloyd successfully defended his firm, proving they were using modified machines long before Eibel had lodged his patent.

In 1910 United Newspapers Ltd was formed with Edward Lloyd Jr as director, to buy Lloyd's newspapers, thus keeping this side of their business separate from that of papermaking. At the same time Edward Lloyd Ltd was formed – the Sittingbourne mill had become the largest in the world. The company had capital of £1,270,000, the largest papermaking concern the industry had ever seen.

Prior to the First World War production at the Sittingbourne mill steadily rose until there were seventeen papermaking machines in full use. Lloyds then turned their attentions to building a dock for ocean-going vessels at Ridham on the Swale, north of

Paper loaded on to carts at Sittingbourne Mill. *(Bowater Paper Organisation Ltd)*

Rear view of Sittingbourne Mill. *(Bowater Paper Organisation Ltd)*

Milton. Milton Creek was starting to silt up and was far too shallow for vessels of any significant size. Connecting the dock to the Sittingbourne mill was a light gauge steam railway. As it crossed the streets around the head of Milton Creek it ran across a reinforced concrete viaduct some 2,805 ft long.

Increased production in the early twentieth century had had an adverse effect. Paper production requires a constant supply of fresh, clean water and when the water from the original stream became insufficient an alternative source had to be found. A suitable supply was found at the Meades in Milton where, owing to the geology of the area, wells had to be drilled into the subterranean reservoir and the water piped into the mill.

Like brickmaker George Smeed, Lloyds looked after the welfare of its workers, and with no hospital in the town where injured workers could be treated, the company built its own, the Memorial Hospital, in Bell Road. Workers paid 1*d* per week into the firm's medical scheme, which rose to 3*d* per week after the First World War. They also built a social club in the Avenue of Remembrance and a sports ground in Gore Court Road and made generous donations towards the cost of building the public swimming baths in the Butts and Trinity Hall off Dover Street.

Ridham Dock, in the mid-1950s, where ocean-going vessels unloaded timber for the Kemsley paper mill. *(Bowater Paper Organisation Ltd)*

Such was Frank Lloyd's concern for the welfare of his workers, that as well as building the Memorial Hospital in Bell Road, he also built a social club for them in the Avenue of Remembrance. *(Bowater Paper Organisation Ltd)*

A shortage of wood pulp and an increased demand for paper in the 1920s led to a rapid rise in the cost of paper, but despite the introduction of a three-shift working system in 1919, which went on to become the accepted working practice, the demand for paper far exceeded the mill's capacity. With no further room for expansion, a new site had to be found.

Kemsley Mill

In 1923 Lloyds began building a new mill at Kemsley, north of Milton. It became operational the following year. The grinder house was linked to Ridham Dock by an aerial steel ropeway, which transported the logs into the mill for grinding. It became the first system in England to grind imported timber. When I was a small boy our house faced Kemsley mill, and I can well recall seeing the buckets full of logs arriving at the mill and being dropped on to the log pile.

The paper store could hold 2,000 tons of paper, which was taken to Ridham Dock and shipped to London or exported abroad. The water supply for this new mill was pumped from the Meades and stored in three large concrete ponds, converted from old washbacks that remained from the days when there was a brickfield on the site. By 1927, when Frank Lloyd died, a third machine was installed at Kemsley to supplement its original two, along with a large boiler and generating plant. Between the two mills, Lloyds were now employing over 2,000 people.

Influenced by workers' housing developments in other parts of the country, such as Port Sunlight in Cheshire, Bournville near Birmingham and the new garden town of Welwyn Garden City, Frank Lloyd decided to build a village for his workers – Kemsley. It was initially designed to house 3,500 people, and by the summer of 1927 188 of the planned 750 houses had been built. The houses were to be of several different designs and were grouped in pairs and blocks of three, four, eight and nine. There were four grades of houses adapted to the requirements of the different classes of tenants.

Following the death of Frank Lloyd the business was sold to Sir William Berry, owner of Allied Newspapers Ltd, who had bought Lloyd's newspapers in 1918 and for whom the mills supplied newsprint. In announcing the takeover to his shareholders, Sir William explained that the Sittingbourne and Kemsley mills between them were the largest in the country and were larger than any in the USA or Canada. They had an annual output of 200,000 tons of newsprint. Expansion of the plant continued with more papermaking machines being installed, including, in 1933, the largest in the world, being 320 ft wide. It was capable of producing 1,000 tons of paper per week. A new power plant, groundwork mill and building-board machines were installed at Kemsley.

In the ten years since being sold to Allied Newspapers Ltd the mills had retained the name Lloyds, but in 1936 changed to Bowaters following an amalgamation. By then it

Kemsley paper mill, mid-1950s. The area of the supposed Viking fortress, Castle Rough, can be seen in the foreground. *(Bowater Paper Organisation Ltd)*

was employing over 3,000 workers and producing 6,500 tons of paper per week. So large was the company that at the time of the takeover Lloyds was the largest paper manufacturer, and workers thought that it was Lloyds who were taking over Bowaters rather than the other way round. The new company, Bowater Lloyd Ltd, became the largest newsprint manufacturer in Europe with a combined annual output of over half a million tons of newsprint; over 60 per cent of Britain's total.

The Second World War brought restrictions on the quantity of newsprint that could be produced and only the Kemsley mill continued producing it. Sittingbourne concentrated on other papermaking operations such as producing Kraft corrugated card, a versatile product made of a sheet of corrugated paper sandwiched between two sheets of smooth paper, which made an incredibly strong piece of cardboard. It was ideal for making boxes for stores, such as ammunition and shells. The first contract for these containers was for one to hold 4½in artillery shells. Between 1935 and 1940 Lloyds supplied 75 per cent of this material to a firm of corrugated paper and box manufacturers, and in 1944 took over the firm completely. By 1945 Bowater had made 10,542,577 containers and other items from Kraft board, including 42,599 disposable

Kemsley paper mill, c. 1930. In the foreground is what must be Burley's brickfield. To the left is the hop field, remembered by many locals. Castle Rough is to the right just below the mill itself. *(Sittingbourne Heritage Museum)*

jettison fuel tanks for aircraft. These had to be built in the Kemsley mill engineering works and at other firms.

At the end of the war everyone tried to get back to normal as quickly as possible, but there was a widespread fear of unemployment. While the men were away fighting women took their places in the mill, and once the men returned they were not happy about giving up their jobs. To allay the fears of unemployment, Bowater secured a lucrative contract with the United States in 1948 to supply newsprint, as well as developing Waxwrap paper and Flexible packaging. At Kemsley the company started to develop insulation board by using the old straw pulping equipment and bleaching system. By 1955 a report on the state of the town's industry showed that Bowater was the largest employer with nearly 5,000 workers, of whom 10 per cent were women, and wages averaged at £12 per week.

In the 1960s there was a drop in demand for newsprint, but by then the Sittingbourne mill was specialising in coated papers of different sorts. History was made in 1967 when a new regular rail freight service started bringing liquid china clay in bulk from Cornwall to the Sittingbourne mill where it was used to coat the paper needed for illustrated and colour productions. In earlier years china clay had been transported by sailing barge. However, in 1967 many mill workers lost their jobs when some machines were closed down. It appeared that the papermaking boom years were over. The introduction of a computerised system in 1973, the most advanced in the papermaking world at the time, led to even more job losses. But there was a light at the end of the tunnel when, in 1977, the company announced plans to develop and modernise the two mills. Despite a £2½ million scheme to protect the mills' future, a lack of orders forced more layoffs and the workforce fell to just 800.

In the late 1980s Bowater sold the Sittingbourne and Kemsley mills to a New Zealand firm, Fletcher Challenge. The old mill was still occupied by the Sittingbourne Paper Co., part of UK Paper Ltd; pulp continued to arrive in lorries from countries as far afield as Finland, Spain and America. In 1991 Mr Rundell, speaking on behalf of the Sittingbourne Paper Co., announced that the company was in the process of installing a new high-cost papermaking plant. It appeared that papermaking, unlike the other previous large-scale industries of the town of the past 150 years, was set to go forward into the twenty-first century. Unfortunately, by May of the following year, a national and international recession started to affect the industry in general and the parent company, Fletcher Challenge, was in financial difficulty. Plans were announced that a packaging machine at Sittingbourne that produced 50,000 tons per year would be shut down with the loss of 100 jobs. But improvements at the Kemsley mill, including the installation of a revolutionary new multi-million pound machine capable of using recycled paper products as the raw material, made the future look a little brighter.

The Downside of Papermaking

While the papermaking industry at the Sittingbourne and Kemsley mills made a sizeable contribution to the town's economy and became the area's largest employer in the twentieth century, it was not without its downside. It has to be said that the mills were responsible for much of the pollution of the town. One of the earliest complaints was made as far back as 1878 by people living near the Sittingbourne mill, who expressed concerns about the smoke, fine ash and sulphuric fumes belching from its chimneys. By 1892, as no improvements had been made, the residents of Milton again petitioned the mill owners about the smoke nuisance. The mill owners put the blame on the inferior quality of the coal they were having to use because of a coal crisis in the north of England.

The smell of a heavily polluted Milton Creek has long been the butt of many jokes about the town. It's a problem that was first noticed in 1895. Despite the Milton Creek Conservatory Board being set up to manage and control the use of the waterway, the problem did not go away. As time went by it slowly got worse. When the tide was low and the wind was in the east, a smell resembling that of bad eggs swept across the whole area, sometimes as far away as Tunstall and Borden. A campaign was launched in the mid-1960s to get rid of the awful smell, and in 1974 a survey by P.M. Bailey was declared the winner in a National Environment Competition. It suggested that Milton Creek was the worst polluted area, not only in Kent, but in the whole of the south of England. Damning evidence indeed.

This marked increase in noticeable pollution was not, however, wholly attributable to the paper mills. With the decline in the number of barges and boats using the Creek and with no fast-flowing streams to purge it, meant that the waterway started to silt up. According to official statistics issued by Bowater at the time, the Sittingbourne mill produced 35,000 gallons of impure water per hour. The amount of cellulose fibre was reduced owing to public pressure and by 1973 the fibre loss was down to less than 1 per cent, whereas 3 per cent was more common elsewhere. Other constituents that were discharged with the water included china clay, dyes and acids, depending on the type of paper being produced at the time.

Before the Creek was dredged, layers of pollutants up to 6 in deep had built up on areas of the Creek bed, especially in its upper reaches, which were only covered by high spring tides. These layers had the texture of soggy cardboard, and suspended solids that were deposited along the banks of the Creek built up and encroached on the main channel. Areas constantly washed by the tides quickly became coated in a thick, greasy, corrosive deposit. From before the Second World War efforts had been made by the mill owners to filter the water to retain as much of the fibre as possible for reuse. In 1971 Bowater installed a flocculating clarifier, a machine that with the aid of chemicals thickened the effluent solids so that the sludge could easily be removed and prevented from entering the Creek. It greatly improved the situation, and after many years the characteristic smell that had once been one of the infamous Seven Stinks of Milton was but a mere shadow of its former self. By 1991 the mill owners had spent over £4 million to meet new European Union targets to clean up the discharged waste water. In 1994 the National Rivers Authority announced that a new waste treatment plant was to be built at Kemsley mill, which would receive effluent by pipe from the Sittingbourne mill, ensuring that Milton Creek would be cleaner than ever.

The Sittingbourne and Kemsley Light Railway

In 1969, after almost seventy years of continual use, the narrow-gauge railway system linking the Sittingbourne mill to Kemsley and Ridham Dock was declared redundant in the face of a more efficient system of road transport. It looked as though another piece of our local heritage was set to be lost, but it was saved by the Light Railway Club of

The Sittingbourne terminus of the Sittingbourne and Kemsley Light Railway. To the right is the *Melior*, built in 1924, and in the centre, the *Superb*. *(East Kent Gazette)*

Great Britain, which was offered it at a peppercorn rent. Much work was needed to restore the rolling stock and trackside facilities, but a dedicated group of volunteers took on the task, and today the Sittingbourne and Kemsley Light Railway operates during the summer months and at special times such as Christmas with great success. It's one of the area's main tourist attractions.

EIGHT
Boats and Barges

A sizeable part of the local economy has long been generated by Milton's position on the Creek. It was not necessarily the lawful trades that brought wealth to Milton Creek in the Middle Ages, or the illegal import of brandy, gin, silk and tobacco, but the smuggling of wool. Since the time of Edward III the export of fleeces from coastal regions had been prohibited. Fleeces were highly prized by the merchants of Lombardy, whose bankers financed the wars of English monarchs. It was these fleeces smuggled out of the Swale ports that brought great wealth to Milton. One of the earliest references to the importance of the Creek is contained in a register dated 1566 and compiled for the war with Scotland. It records that there were twenty-nine vessels at Sittingbourne and Milton, the largest being of 26 tons. Most of these were probably fishing boats, although some could have been small coastal trading vessels known as navicules.

Milton was at the centre of an important fishing industry at that time and over 10 per cent of the wills published referred to ownership of such vessels. Most referred to the vessels as being dredging boats, which indicates that they were used to catch shellfish such as oysters. In 1528 boat owner Garrard Johnson bequeathed 40 bushels of oysters at 'his burying day'.

The Coming of the Hoys

By the mid-seventeenth century Milton was handling over 10 per cent of the grain shipment from Kent to London. In a six-month period in 1700 it is recorded that there were seventy-eight outgoing cargoes, which included oats, wheat, malt, hops, wool and copperas (possibly blue copperas, or copper sulphate, from Tankerton Bay, Whitstable, Kent). With an increasing commercial market, the Tappenden family established a hoy business on the Creek. Cutter rigged hoys originated in Holland and are first recorded on the Swale in 1568 when Elizabeth I gave sanctuary to some Huguenots from

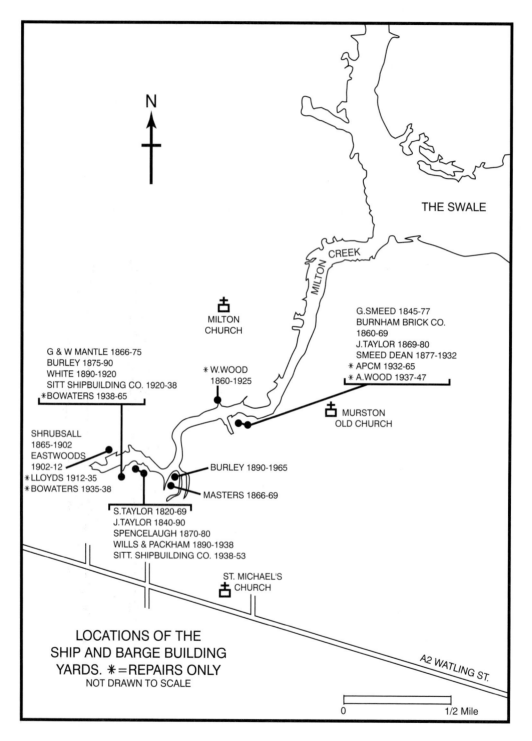

A plan of the ship and barge building yards in Sittingbourne. *(J. Clancy)*

Antwerp at Faversham. These flat-bottomed vessels were ideally suited to carry produce to coastal ports at a time when travel by road was difficult and dangerous. Tappenden's business was taken over in 1733 following the family's success in diversifying into carrying cash for wealthy clients, credit policies and loans at interest. The new business developed into the Faversham Bank. Hoys continued to operate in and out of Milton Creek until 1905.

One of the last big coasting hoys was the boomsail-rigged *Henry Everist*, a vessel named after a barge-fleet owner of the same name. She was acquired by George Smeed whose original intention was to re-rig her like a traditional 'boomie barge', but before he could issue the instruction, his master shipwright, Frederick Sollitt, cut her in half and rebuilt the hull. She ended up as a three-masted schooner barge called the *Ellen Smeed* in 1872.

Prior to 1830 only small vessels could reach Crown Quay and Milton Wharf and that was only on the high spring tides. Larger vessels had to anchor at the mouth of the Creek and discharge their cargo into lighters. Murston was starting to emerge as a port and it had the advantage of having deeper draft facilities.

Shipbuilding

A report of 1729 mentions a coastal hoy with a capacity of '400 quarter of corn under her deck' being built at Milton. Other references to shipbuilding on the Creek come from the Milton burial register of the 1750s and an order dated 1799 for a vessel to be built for a firm from Suffolk. This was to be a new industry for Milton.

Milton Creek remained a haven for its fishing fleet, coastal hoys, shipbuilding and repair yards until the mid-nineteenth century when George Smeed started using Thames spritsail sailing barges to transport his bricks and cement. It was like transforming a road from a quiet country lane into a busy motorway. The barges had traded to Milton Creek in a small way during the eighteenth century, but because of their unique design, being large flat-bottomed vessels with leeboards, they were ideal for the shallow conditions in the Creek. The barges only needed a 4 ft draft, and despite their size, they could be crewed by just two people who could easily lower the 40 ft mainmast and 30 ft topmast when they approached a bridge, so they were ideal to sail up the Thames into London. They were basic in design, and during the French Wars it was found they could be built cheaply from second-hand materials bought from the dockyards. If the waterways can be described as being the motorways of the nineteenth century, then the barges were most definitely the equivalent of today's juggernauts; they carried anything and everything.

Smeed was a great believer in self-sufficiency, and boatbuilding, particularly barges, was a logical next step in his overall operation. His first shipyard was at Adelaide Dock

Crown Quay, Sittingbourne, with a couple of barges awaiting a favourable tide. The vessel nearest the camera is the *Sir Wilfred Lawson*. (C. Deamer)

and later Murston Wharf, from where he launched seventy-nine sailing vessels including a large number of schooner, barquentine and barque-rigged sailing barges, the largest of which was said to be capable of carrying 800 tons of cargo. By cleverly combining the rig of a conventional coastal vessel with the hull design and leeboards of a small sailing barge, it allowed the barges to carry a large cargo into shallow draft ports. Many of Smeed's largest vessels were engaged in the coal trade, supplying either gas coal or coking coal to the small south-east coastal ports. The traditional sailing collier was a deep-draft vessel, but Smeed's barges could carry twice as much cargo and use a smaller crew. The colliers also needed to be loaded with chalk ballast for the return trip; the barges did not.

One of the first barges Smeed owned was built in 1837 and he named it *George*. With it came a small schooner built in Milton Creek in 1858, which he named *Eliza*, after his wife. Successive vessels bore the names of his children. It became a tradition for all future barge owners to name their vessels after their families and those of their directors and principal staff, a tradition that continued until the last barge, *Youngarth* (after Garth Doubleday), was built in 1913.

The first barge that Smeed built was the *Three Sisters* in 1845. Her captain was William Pretty who later died when he was swept overboard, having been struck by the tiller when his vessel collided with the *George* off Murston. This was the second barge to be named *George*, which was built at Adelaide Dock in 1852.

Also built at Adelaide Dock in that year were the *Lucretia* and the *Georgiana*, the first of three vessels to bear that name. Georgiana was the daughter of Smeed's barge yard manager, John Epps, and the third vessel to bear that name was named in honour of her twenty-first birthday. These barges were typically 60 ft long and 14 ft wide. It was not uncommon for them to trade as far as the north of England or across the Channel to the continent. It was on such a cross-Channel trip that the first *Georgiana* was lost off Rye while carrying a cargo of cement on 2 June 1860. She was seen foundering from the shore with her captain, Fred Love, and the mate, John Goulding, both lashed to the mast. In such a heavy sea the lifeboat could not be launched; in those days the lifeboat was little more than a large, open rowing boat. As dawn broke there was no sign of the barge or its occupants.

Cement was not an uncommon cargo to be shipped to the continent, but on one occasion the continental brokers had been searching for a return cargo for one barge and the best they could find was a consignment of Belgian cement!

George Smeed was not the only barge owner or builder in this area. He owned around half of the fleet of upwards of a hundred such vessels that were based at Milton Creek. Only thirty years earlier it had numbered just nine barges. There was probably no other Creek in the country that had a similar amount of traffic regularly using it. And it continued to grow. The Mercantile Navy list of 1872 shows there were 190 Milton-built vessels then, but by 1886 the fleet had grown to 343 and by 1900, 410.

Another firm of shipbuilders on the Creek was the Taylor family, whose yard was at Crown Quay. Stephen Taylor was listed in the census records of 1861 as being a bargebuilder and ropemaker who employed twelve men and seven boys. Two of his sons, Stephen Jr and John, lived nearby and both of them were engaged in the same business. Their sons similarly followed their fathers into the trade. In 1862 the Taylors were building barges for London-based owners as well as local owners such as Burley's. However, barges were not the only vessels they built. In 1871 they launched a 200-ton schooner barge for a London owner and a floating swimming bath surrounded by a deck for changing rooms to be moored at Southend. By 1881 it appears that John Taylor was the only member of this family still employed in shipbuilding with twelve men and four boys.

Soon after the Dolphin Barge Museum was opened, one of the first vessels in for re-rigging was the *Oak*. Here she's looking almost as good as the day she was launched. *(M. Clancy)*

Like George Smeed, fellow brickmakers Wills and Packham could also see sense in maintaining a fleet of barges in which to transport their bricks. Their vessels were known as 'teetotal' barges as each one was named after temperance reformers. Mr Wills had a house built in Park Road, which he named Garfield House. From a lofty turret-room window, he could watch his barges sailing up the Creek.

The size and variety of the boats being built on the Creek gradually increased during the second half of the nineteenth century. For example, in 1858 Stephen Taylor launched a cutter of some 50 tons and seven years later a 150-ton barge for Burley's, followed by a 200-ton schooner. The day books of the Smeed Dean barge yard of the 1890s give an excellent indication of the type of work being carried out. In 1898 agreements were made for two new barges to be built, one for Burley's at a cost of £900 and the other for Mr Wood at £850. As well as building new barges, others came in for repair and maintenance. The *Dick Turpin* needed over £300-worth of repairs, which included £60 for new timber and a further £25 for deepening the vessel. The busiest months in the yard were from June to August when an average of twenty-three barges were repaired.

One of the many quays on Milton Creek. In the centre is one of Lloyd's early steam-driven tugs with its tall funnel. *(Sittingbourne Heritage Museum)*

The slackest time was the winter months between December and February with an average of less than ten. Some vessels would be in for several weeks with a number of different jobs being done, whereas others would require only a single, simple job, so their turn-around period would be quite quick.

The Racing Barges

Two local yards noted for building fast-moving barges which accounted for some good performances in the annual barge races on the Thames and Medway, were Robert Shrubsall and Alfred White Sr. Shrubsall was responsible for building seventy barges in the last thirty years of the nineteenth century, at least nine of which were accredited racing champions. After Robert Shrubsall died in 1901 his yard was taken over by brickmakers Eastwoods whose foreman shipwright, Alex Styles, was responsible for launching a further ten barges between 1902 and 1908. Eastwoods retained the yard for maintenance work until 1912, and then moved on to Otterham Quay at Rainham.

Shrubsall's old yard was near Prentis Quay, opposite which was the yard of Alfred White Sr. He also specialised in building fast-moving vessels from 1895 until 1910, and like Robert Shrubsall had several racing champions. Eventually, both of these yards were taken over by Lloyds and then Bowaters for the maintenance of their lighters. With so

Peter Renton of the Dolphin Sailing Barge Museum proudly displays the long-lost racing pennant won by Burley's sailing barge, *Northdown*, in the Medway barge races of 1929. Measuring 25 ft long, it would have been proudly flown from the top of the mast on race days (see picture on page 119). Unfortunately it was the last time that a sailing barge from Burley's yard won a championship. She was built in Whitstable by Anderson, Rigden and Perkins in 1924 and sold to Chas Burley. In 1980 she was given to a museum in France. However, it is not known what happened to her next. *(Kent Messenger)*

much activity going on, a somewhat optimistic guidebook published in Edwardian times enthusiastically suggested the possibility that Milton Creek might soon become a second Clyde.

A New Type of Barge

One major change to the range of vessels being built at Smeed's Adelaide Dock yard came about as a result of a strike by shipwrights in November 1862, who demanded a five-day week. When their demand was refused they sought work elsewhere, except for two loyal workers who had not struck. Smeed was forced to look for a new master shipwright to take over the management of the yard. He found the ideal person in Frederick Sollitt, a foreman shipwright at Chatham Dockyard. He had considerable knowledge of building flat-bottomed vessels, and this expertise, together with Smeed's business acumen, produced a new breed of vessel.

The problem that faced many owners of vessels trading to the north-east coal ports was that Blythe, Seaham and Hartlepool were yet to be developed as deep-water ports and Sunderland, Shields and Newcastle-upon-Tyne had sand bars across the river mouths. To get over these, vessels could only be part-loaded at the quayside and the rest of the cargo loaded once the vessel was over the sand bar. On their return to the Kent ports, only small vessels could negotiate the shallow twisting creeks. Ideally what was needed was a large vessel to carry a maximum load, yet small enough to negotiate the navigational problems.

To get around this Sollitt developed a large flat-bottomed vessel similar to existing Dutch vessels. A three-masted version of this had been built at Battersea in 1854, and in the same year smaller single-masted versions called 'flats' were built at Faversham. Sollitt took the design a step further. His barges were constructed below the waterline in much the same way as a Thames sailing barge, but it was above the waterline where the fundamental differences were introduced. The stern, for example, was finished with an overhanging elliptical counter with a curved stem from which protruded a raked bowsprit. The bulwarks were high and incorporated forward bowboards and quarter boards continuing as stern boards. Above the waterline there was little to distinguish them from the traditional sailing barge. They were three-masted with square yards set on the foremast and Sollitt described it as a schooner barge. His first such vessel was the *Seven Sisters* (Smeed had seven daughters), which was launched by Miss Eliza Smeed on 1 April 1862. She measured 125 ft by 23½ ft and had a hold of some 9½ ft deep. Her carrying capacity was 300 tons. By comparison, the smaller ketch, or boomie barge, similar to the Thames spritsail sailing barge in design, which was commonly built at Milton Creek, was designed to carry only about 150 tons, being a much smaller vessel.

From the schooner barge developed the even larger clipper schooner. She was enormous with an overall length of 140 ft. Her beam, or width, was almost 28 ft and her hold was 13 ft deep. Named the *Eliza Smeed*, she was launched on 14 March 1865 after taking a year to build. She was put under the command of Capt Edwin Sellen, who as soon as she was fitted out took the empty vessel to the north-east to collect a cargo of coal destined for Rochester. Earlier, in May 1862, Captain Sellen had claimed a record in the collier schooner *Fanny* by completing three round trips between Sittingbourne and Hartlepool in the month.

Even bigger vessels were to follow. Almost as soon as the *Eliza Smeed* was launched a barque-rigged barge, to be named the *George Smeed*, was undergoing construction. She was designed to carry over 700 tons of coal and was 156 ft long. Her beam was 30 ft and the depth of the hold was 15 ft. To achieve a similar cargo-carrying capacity, a conventional round-hulled vessel would have needed a hold with a depth of 18 ft. Being such a large vessel, she was difficult to launch. Mrs Smeed tried to launch the vessel on 8 November 1866, but it stayed fast, refusing to float off. Shipyard workers had to wait for an exceptionally high tide two days later.

The largest barque-rigged barge made here was the 494-ton *Esther Smeed* in 1868 and she could carry over 800 tons of cargo. One of her regular trips was to the west of Ireland for which her rigging was cut down to the size of the more manageable three-masted schooner. Later she traded on charter to the Baltic when George Andrews's son George Jr pleaded with his parents to allow him to join the ship as a boy to the captain, James Bennett. On 30 September 1878 the *Esther Smeed* foundered on the northern side of Gotska Sandon, a small island between the Gulf of Riga and Stockholm. At a

In 1995 the *Celtic* came to the Dolphin Barge Museum for extensive repairs. *(Barry Kinnersley)*

subsequent hearing Bennett had his master's certificate suspended for twelve months and the mate, William Hambly, lost his ticket for six months. At first glance it may seem that these vessels would not be suitable for work in a harsh environment such as the Baltic, but they were, and in December 1879 Capt William King, the then owner of the *George Smeed*, sold her to Norwegian owners.

As these larger vessels became more and more popular, Sollitt broke up many of Smeed Dean's smaller barges and used the timber to build vessels like the *Emily Smeed* in 1872. The last of these super-barges that Sollitt was responsible for was the *Sarah Smeed* that was built in March 1874. Twenty-six years later, however, the firm launched just one more big barge, the 'boomie' *SD*, known to many as the 'Sudden Death'.

The Brotherhood of Bargemen

Following a strike by London dockers in 1889 the Society For the Protection of Bargemen and Watermen was constituted to protect its members' interests in future pay negotiations. The bargemen of Sittingbourne and Milton were among the first to join this new union by forming Unity Lodge No. 2 with between 400 and 500 members. It was designed to be a social and spiritual organisation.

Formed by the vicar of St Michael's church and editor of *The Bargeman* magazine, the Revd Mr Parry-Evans, the Brotherhood had a clubhouse in Crown Quay Lane, which was opened in 1921, on a piece of ground opposite what is now the Barge public house. Members were entitled to wear an anchor-shaped emblem on their watch chain and fly a pennant bearing the letters BB at the masthead of their vessel. After the opening ceremony the bargemen processed to Bowes Park, a sports ground in what is now the triangle of Bell Road and Greyshott Close, for an afternoon of entertainment arranged by the bargemen for their friends and family. Mr Toms, a Salvation Army official who was himself a bargeman, led the procession. The clubhouse was demolished in about 1942 and the public house opposite, then the White Hart, has been renamed the Barge in the bargemen's honour.

Smeed Dean Ltd was always recognised as being a good firm to work for, no matter in which branch you were engaged. George Smeed was a fair man who stood no nonsense from his workers. One example of his generosity is the Bargemen's Benefit Club that he ran. For 6*d* per week members could claim sick pay at 10*s* for the first thirteen weeks, 5*s* for the next thirteen weeks and 2*s* 6*d* for the succeeding twenty-six. In the event of the death of a member £5 would be paid to his dependant or if it were the death of a member's wife or a single member's mother who had been dependant upon him, the sum of £2 10*s*. There was always a share-out at Christmas, and mates of the barges who were members qualified for a reduction of 2*d* in their weekly payments.

Following the sale of Smeed Dean to APCM in 1927 two former directors, George Andrews and his son Harold, were left with six barges with no home base. They sought suitable accommodation with the idea of building up to a fleet of about twenty to twenty-five vessels that could be used for general freight conveyance. They found exactly what they were looking for in the near bankrupt, independently run boatyard of the Sittingbourne Shipbuilding Co. Ltd. It was near the head of the Creek in the former White's yard. Harold Andrews acquired the business in 1930 and another former Smeed Dean employee, Sid Ellis, came to join him, bringing into the partnership a few more barges. Although the partnership was never legally binding, it was known as Ellis and Andrews and all their barges flew the same bob, or pennant.

After acquiring the Sittingbourne Shipbuilding Co., Harold Andrews retained the services of the company's founder, Mr H.W. Harvey, an independent marine surveyor, as his technical adviser. He also brought in Smeed Dean's former foreman shipwright, Vic Horsford, and several members of his gang.

From the early 1930s right up until the 1950s the company rebuilt, converted and motorised many of the well-known local barges. They also built versions of the East

The *Cambria* undergoing restoration at the Dolphin Barge Museum in 1998. The *Cambria* was the last barge to trade purely under sail and was the last to carry cargo in Milton Creek. She is now owned by the Cambria Trust. *(Barry Kinnersley)*

Coast barge-yacht, a scaled down version of the Thames spritsail sailing barge, with the hold being fitted out with accommodation. Almost from the day of its inception the company held valuable government contracts for the construction of auxiliary Naval craft, and following the expansion of this particular programme at the outbreak of the Second World War the adjacent larger premises of Wills and Packham Ltd were acquired. At the end of the war, with much-improved transport links now in place by road and rail, transport by barges was gradually being phased out, as it was no longer practical or financially viable. The death knell of the barge had been sounded. The yard's main buildings were given over to other uses and by 1952–3 the premises of the former Sittingbourne Shipbuilding Co. had become a warehousing business.

At the same time three other small shipyards run by Bowater's, Burley and APCM also closed down for the same reason. Apart from it being the end of the days of the barge, it was also the end of the Creek being used for commercial purposes. For many years the papermaking industry had been depriving it of a natural flow of clean, clear water, and with no vessels using it the Creek became a polluted, silted-up waterway, which was to become an eyesore to the town.

The Change to Tugs and Lighters

By 1946 sailing-barge traffic on Milton Creek had virtually ceased. There was still cargo going in and out but it was mostly by tugs and lighters. At one time papermakers Bowater-Lloyd, who had gone over to powered craft in about 1912 following the bargemen's strike, owned the only lighters in the Creek. These lighters could carry about 200 tons and most were built of wood, although some were of steel, and the crews could live aboard them. Their cargoes were varied. They carried wood pulp to the local paper mills and transported the finished product to wherever it was needed. China clay from Cornwall was loaded into them from larger ships at Ridham Dock and lightered up to Sittingbourne paper mill. Brickmaker Chas Burley had a motor vessel, the *Queen Philippa*, which loaded rubbish herself and towed two lighters that were also fully loaded.

Dolphin Sailing Barge Museum

After more than a century of being a major local industry little now remains of the barge yards, quays and wharves that once dominated the banks of Milton Creek. They have all been swept away and built upon by modern industrial developments. One tantalising glimpse does remain and it should be jealously guarded and cherished by all of those who care for our past. I refer to the Dolphin Sailing Barge Museum in Crown Quay Lane.

It is situated in what was formerly Burley's barge yard and the buildings date from about 1890. Many of the upright timbers used in the construction of the forge and sail loft were formerly the tillers of old barges and still bear intricate carvings to prove it. In about 1890 tillers were being discarded in favour of wheels as a means of steering the vessels. The yard became disused and derelict after Burley's sold their last motor barge in the mid-1960s.

In about 1969 an organisation was set up with the aim of leasing, restoring and opening the old barge yard as a working museum. The owners of the site, Bourncrete Concrete Products Ltd, were sympathetic to the cause and agreed to lease it to the group at a peppercorn rent. The museum was formally opened by Cllr Buckey in 1970 and named Dolphin after the brand name of the cement made at the nearby Burley cement works.

After a few troubled years the museum closed owing to operational difficulties and the site started to revert to its

The bow of the *Cambria* during restoration at the Dolphin Sailing Barge Museum in 1998. *(Barry Kinnersley)*

A snowscape of the Dolphin Sailing Barge Museum with the barge *Cambria* tied up to the quay. *(Sketch by Sylvia Hankin)*

former derelict state. Fortunately all was not lost and in 1978–9 a group of London-based barge organisations and some knowledgeable barge owners encouraged and guided the museum officials into reorganising and reopening the yard. In May 1979 Sittingbourne's VC hero, Col. Donald Dean, officially reopened the museum. Col. Dean was a most appropriate choice, being a descendant of George Hambrook Dean, part of the Smeed Dean partnership. He had had a barge named after him, the *Donald*, which was renamed the *VC* after he was awarded that honour for his gallantry in the First World War. Since then the museum has progressed in fine style with an ever-increasing number of exhibits and high-quality exhibition material.

To commemorate the town's long association with the sailing barge, a statue of a bargeman and his dog was erected in Sittingbourne High Street and unveiled by the Mayor of Swale, Cllr E. Madgwick, in June 1996, to commemorate the refurbishment of the High Street. The statue is the work of Jill Tweed FRSB. *(Barry Kinnersley)*

NINE

Minor Industries of the Twentieth Century

As well as the major industries discussed in previous chapters there have been many smaller ones, which, despite their small size and the minimal impact they made upon the local economy, deserve a brief mention. Each has little significant history to speak of, but collectively they form a part of the overall history and heritage of the area and as such should not be overlooked or discounted. At the beginning of the twenty-first century there are few shops left in the High Street that can be considered as long-standing, except perhaps for Dolding's menswear, Blundell's furnishers, Thompsett's fishmongers and Birch's newsagents. (Recently it has been announced that after trading for 142 years the fishmonger's is to close. The shop has been in the Thomsett family since 1903.) These are shops I can remember from my childhood days. I apologise in advance if I have overlooked any others that are worthy of inclusion.

In the nineteenth century there was the Murston chemical works of Couper and Somerville that stood near the gas works. The creosote boiler and tank containing pitch caught fire in 1867, but fortunately the naphtha in barrels was saved. There was another fire later in the same year when newspaper reports described the works as manufacturing pitch, tar, naphtha and other chemicals. Later there was a second chemical plant called Bugges Insecticide Works on the corner of Cryalls Lane and the London Road. Complaints were lodged in 1932 about the fumes emitted from the plant. In 1935 there was a massive fire there. Bugges Insecticide Works had originally been built by Laurance Seager who, during the First World War, had used it as a fruit-pulping station. After the war the well-known jam and marmalade manufacturer Keillers used it for the same purpose as well as jam making. When Bugges took over the premises they enlarged them, employing some twenty to twenty-five people, mainly ex-servicemen.

Keillers were not the only firm processing fruit in the town at this time. During the First World War F.G. Gooding opened a factory in Milton for preserving cherries, followed in 1929 by William Opie who was engaged in much the same operation in Chalkwell Road. At the time the French dominated the glacé cherry market, but

William Opie, after much experimenting, learnt to produce glacé cherries as good as the French; after all, this was a major cherry-growing area.

His father, Bennett, whose name is still used by the business, was a former Cornish tin miner who, following a serious mining accident in 1880, started an egg distribution business from the West Country to London. The business expanded to include selling bacon on behalf of several large firms, and by 1924 glacé cherries as well. At first the company imported expensive French cherries, but William decided it made more sense to find a factory in the heart of the English cherry-growing regions. His search for a suitable site brought him to Sittingbourne. Following the death of Bennett Opie in 1929, William became managing director. The firm has survived to this day as a family-run business, still producing preserved fruit and, more recently, pickles as well.

Another firm processing fruit locally was Dean's jam factory in Bell Road. During the early nineteenth century jam was regarded as a luxury, but following a fall in sugar prices in the 1850s and '60s the jam-making industry started to grow, making fruit-growing more profitable as damaged fruit could be put to good use. The factory began in the nineteenth century by processing fruit from the extensive farmland owned by the Dean family. George Dean was a partner in the brickmaking firm Smeed Dean. In 1915 'Dean's Famous Kentish Jams' were being sent to British troops on the Western Front. By the second half of the twentieth century the premises had been bought firstly by Sharwoods, who produced pickles and chutney, and later, Freshbake Foods. They were closed in the 1980s and today are used as offices of the Swale Housing Association.

There have been several small-scale engineering firms in the town for many years, each brought about, no doubt, by the needs of the barge building, windmill and brickmaking industries. In the 1860s Mr Gardiner opened an iron foundry just off the High Street, and nine years later Mr F. Littlewood established his engineering works at the bottom of Milton Hill. He was a brassfounder and brick mould manufacturer who also repaired machinery; he did a lot of repair work at the Meades windmill. At the same time the East Kent Ironworks was operating, but in the 1930s was taken over by the Stevens family who already had an engineering works at Thurrock in Essex. In its early years this firm had made windlass gear for barges. They opened a machine shop in Crown Quay Lane in 1955 where parts were made for turbines and papermaking machinery. The original premises in Frederick Street were retained as a foundry and pattern-making shop.

Clothing firms have been prominent in the town for a number of years, the first being a collar factory in Ufton Lane on its corner with Addington Road, a road long known to locals as 'Collar Factory Hill'. It opened in 1912 and employed a total of 100 people including girls from the age of fourteen. Another was Posner's, which opened a brand-new factory in Staplehurst Road in the 1950s; this continued under various owners until the 1990s.

Lowes Dog Biscuit factory lay to the west of the town in Wellwinch Road until the 1970s and was close to Export Packing Services, which opened in the 1950s. Frederick

Women workers making jam at Dean's jam factory. *(Sittingbourne Library)*

Workers packing the finished product at Dean's jam factory. *(Sittingbourne Library)*

Dean's jam factory in Bell Road. The premises are now used as the office of Swale Housing Association. *(Sittingbourne Library)*

Women workers in Bennett Opie's glacé cherry factory. *(Bennett Opie Ltd)*

Lowe was a Devonian who as a young man had trained field dogs. He was so successful that he took it up as a career, entering dogs in field trials as well as breeding and selling them and acting as a judge. He moved to Frinsted in the 1880s where he started manufacturing Carta Carna dog biscuits, two words taken from Hindustani for 'dogs' food'. At the turn of the twentieth century Lowe moved to Bobbing Place and opened his factory in Wellwinch Road. The dog biscuits became an international favourite and for many years, a sign on Sittingbourne railway station proclaimed that this was 'the home of Lowe's dog biscuits'. The firm's trademark was the head of a dog, Ben of Keppen, that Frederick Lowe had bred himself. During the First World War the factory was adapted to make biscuits for the troops with a weekly output of 50 tons. Frederick Lowe died in September 1930 at the age of eighty-three.

A common enough sight on the roads around Sittingbourne and district is coaches bearing the name Chalkwell Coaches. The company began life as Island Luxury Coaches, set up by Harry Eglinton in 1931. To step into the company's office is like stepping into a massive archive; Harry never threw any document away, no matter how trivial or insignificant it might have seemed. The documents give a wonderfully detailed history of the company. For example, in April 1933 Sittingbourne Football Club hired a fourteen-seater coach to take them to a match at Aylesford for the sum of £1 10s. Later that same month the team played at Erith when the coach hire was £2 5s. A slightly more expensive trip was one to Wembley in the previous year, which cost £7 9s 6d. Harry even kept the receipt for his first motorcycle, which cost £28 10s. His passion for hoarding things extended to spare parts for his coaches, and although not required for many years as the coaches were sold or disposed of, these spare parts are now much in demand by collectors of vintage vehicles and transport museums.

The Eglintons were a typical East End family and Harry's father, Joe, was a butcher. Rather than follow in his father's footsteps, when he left school at fourteen Harry became a cabinetmaker, but after buying his first motorcycle became an apprentice motor mechanic. The garage where he worked ran a fleet of taxis and chauffeur-driven cars, so Harry spent long periods of time away from home chauffeuring. His move to coaches came following a request to repair two old charabancs. He was immediately hooked and was soon seeking one of his own. His first was a 1929 Gilford 166ST, a twenty-six-seater with a Duple body, which cost Harry £800. With it he began an express service from Stoke Newington, London, to Sheerness – where he moved. It was to be short lived, as road service licensing was being introduced by the traffic commissioners, and because Harry was unable to show a period of prior operation during 1930 he was not given a licence, but he was not deterred. By 1932 Harry had moved from Sheerness to Sittingbourne because, as he put it, 'it was conveniently placed to reach everywhere else'. In 1938 the company bought the garage in Chalkwell Road where it remains to this day. Before it had been owned by the London and Provincial Produce Transport Ltd, which transported local produce to Covent Garden market.

The Second World War had a profound effect on the business, as the army requisitioned all the newer coaches and the older ones had to be sold as the market dwindled. The garage building was also taken over, and after being given a reinforced concrete roof it was used as a civil defence headquarters and ambulance station. In making the best of a bad job Harry joined the civil defence as a motor transport officer. He often drove the ambulance and saw his fair share of the action, being first on the scene at Detling Aerodrome when it was bombed, and also at Canterbury when the city was attacked.

After the war, with little prospect of buying any new coaches, Harry took up taxi driving. The few coaches that were coming on to the market commanded prohibitively high prices and were usually snapped up by the larger operators. By 1948 things had started to change and Harry was able to buy a twenty-nine-seater Bedford OB Duple Vista coach. It remained the mainstay of the business throughout the 1950s, and after being sold in 1960 was snapped up by a number of vintage coach enthusiasts who cared for it, restored it and used it for promotion and TV work. The distinctive livery of Parson's Longacre red with a white flash and black mudguards was adopted, but when later this colour became obsolete the nearest match that could be found was Ford Monaco red. Right up to the time of his death in 1994 Harry continued to take an active interest in the business, taking every opportunity to drive and help out. He was almost certainly the last survivor of his generation of Kent coach operators who saw passenger transport develop from horse-drawn trams to today's large super-coaches. Today the business is in the hands of Harry's son, Clive, who continues with the high level of service set by his father. One other local firm of coach operators that I remember from my childhood is Smith's Coaches who operated from the top of Hythe Road. If my memory serves me right, they operated from about the 1950s, and I understand they ceased trading in the 1990s.

The second half of the twentieth century has seen the development of several small industrial trading estates. By 1972 there were three, the London Road Trading Estate on Hollybank Hill, the Trinity Trading Estate in Milton and the latest, the Sittingbourne Industrial Park, which covers most of the former industrial area of Sittingbourne. Following the closure of the Murston cement works, the Eurolink Industrial Estate began to blot out the former Smeed Dean brickfields. It is indicative of the changing nature of the urban economy that firms like Concrete Pipes Ltd, one of many small-scale businesses, continues to manufacture concrete products in Milton, despite the fact that large-scale concrete manufacturers are long gone. The town's economy is no longer dominated by single industries as it was in the nineteenth century by brickmaking and in the early twentieth by papermaking.

There was once a laundry, in the alley beside what is now Blundell's toyshop. Known as the Queen's Laundry, it is something of a mystery in that no one seems to know anything about its history despite repeated requests in the local press. In 1998 a set of

Hard at work in the Queen's Laundry that once stood near the Queen's cinema, formerly Vallance and Payne's brewery, up the alley beside Blundell's toy shop. *(Sittingbourne Heritage Museum)*

glass negatives of views of the interior of a laundry came up for auction in Norfolk. The purchaser discovered they were of the Sittingbourne laundry and sent them to town historian Cllr Peter Morgan who began investigating its history. He drew a blank. It seems that no one knows exactly when it opened, but I remember that it closed down in the 1950s, probably at a time when domestic washing machines were starting to become more readily available. After its closure the building was used as a factory, but it later burnt down, a fate shared by the adjoining Queen's cinema building, which was a discotheque in later years. Of equal mystery is the laundry's name. Next to it was the Queen's cinema. Both buildings have now long been demolished and a car park occupies the site. Even elderly residents of the town cannot help in solving this mystery, but each clearly remembers the laundry being there in their childhood in the early 1900s.

Throughout the town there are tangible reminders of those who once dominated our local economy in the naming of new roads. There's Dean Road, Watson's Hill, Eastwood Road and Smeed Close. Other roads remind us of past industries like Brewery Road, Gas Road, Kiln Close, Mill Court, Millfield, Mill Way, Oyster Close, Saffron Way and Tannery Court. I wonder how many residents of those roads know exactly what lies behind the naming of their road?

TEN

The Changing Face of Sittingbourne

Sittingbourne is now vastly different from how it was at the start of the last millennium. The town has grown from an insignificant little hamlet that modestly served the needs of passing travellers, to the sizeable multi-functioned conurbation it is today. It seized every opportunity to improve and expand, firstly by catering for the needs of pilgrims and other travellers, and later adapting its inns to accommodate the needs of passing stagecoaches. The coming of the railway further improved Sittingbourne's economy and it led to a period of rapid growth and extensive industrialisation. As the population increased, with many people being drawn to the area by the prospect of well-paid, steady employment, housing became a priority. The electrification of the railway line in the 1950s brought London within a commutable distance from Sittingbourne and it almost became a dormitory town. The railway station was enlarged to cope with the additional traffic, which was expected to double as more and more city workers made their home here and more houses were needed for this new sector of our population. After much heated discussion, and sometimes bitter wrangling, Sittingbourne and Milton Regis eventually became one single district in 1931 following the amalgamation of the two separate town councils to form Sittingbourne and Milton Urban District Council. It further increased in size with the addition of Murston. The surrounding agricultural land was slowly eroded away as new housing estates were created following the Housing Act of 1919.

The Housing Programme

As the town grew there was a dire need for more houses. In 1925 the town's housing inspector reported that of the 1,965 houses in the district, 237 had two or more families living in them. Overcrowding was a serious problem. The council agreed to support the Owner-Occupier Scheme whereby they granted a subsidy of £75 per house and advanced 90 per cent of its valuation.

In complying with the Housing Act, Sittingbourne UDC built fifty houses in Bell Road and Chilton Avenue; Milton UDC built eight at London Road, and, there were a further eight in Murston. Work was completed by 1923, and following a short lull Sittingbourne UDC built a further twenty houses at Glovers Crescent in 1926 for sale to the tenants. Similar development followed in 1928 at Trotts Hall Gardens when thirty-two houses were built, but it still was not enough to solve the overcrowding problem. South Avenue Estate and Barrow Grove Estate followed in 1929 and Milton Council began work on the Vicarage Orchard Estate. It was the start of bigger schemes to come.

Following the amalgamation of the two councils, work began on the Elm Grove and Quinton Estates. With additional houses being added to the Vicarage Orchard and Elm Grove Estates in 1936–7, it brought the number of houses built by the local authority in the inter-war years to 712. In 1933 the council took over the mortgage for thirty-one houses in Ruins Barn Road, which had earlier been granted to a private developer by the former Milton Rural District Council, but as it had failed to make the repayments the mortgage had been withdrawn.

Despite this frenzied activity there were still 853 people awaiting rehousing. The council was concerned about the slum conditions in some parts of the town and the high rents being charged by greedy landlords. More had to be done and several private developers also contributed to the town's housing stock. In 1933 semi-detached houses with garages were built on the Westlands Estate and two years later Wraight's developed the Hawthorn Orchard Estate. It was rumoured in 1935 that an estate might be built at Gore Court Park, the former home of George Smeed, but the council scotched the idea, saying that they would prefer to keep the land for public use. It later became King George's Playing Field.

The housing development programme planned that the new houses would be distributed over a wide area in various parts of the district, enabling tenants to live close to their workplace. With the declaration of war in 1939 the programme had to be put on hold until 1944 when the council purchased a 36-acre site between Ufton Lane and College Road. Work started in 1946 with the infrastructure being built by prisoners of war.

In 1945 the council acquired the 58-acre site that was to become the Canterbury Road Estate, the second of the council's large developments. Building work commenced at the end of 1947 and the Minister of Health, Sir William S. Douglas KCB, KBE, officially opened the first house on 11 August 1948. With work progressing well on the Canterbury Road Estate, the council pressed ahead with the development of what was to become known as the Homewood Avenue Estate. With the roads and sewers in place, building work began in April 1951.

Before the whole area was demolished and swept away in the 1970s as part of the slum clearance programme, this was the corner of Flushing Street and Mill Street. The pub was the Waterman's Arms, and to the right of the first-floor window a plaque can clearly be seen showing the arms of the Honourable Company of Fruiterers. It is dated 1662 and bears the letters 'ReED'. Two tenements in Milton once belonged to this company. Was this one of them? Kingsmill Road was to the right and one of its houses bore a terracotta tablet bearing the date 1644. *(East Kent Gazette)*

The next major estate to be constructed was on the 27-acre site that had formerly been part of Burley's brickfield in Milton. It would link Milton church to the town once again. The course of an ancient stream that flowed from the Meades along Vicarage Road and North Street to Church Marshes caused more than a few problems for engineers installing soil and surface drainage. Called North Court Estate, it was scheduled to have 300 dwellings, which owing to new designs based on the Ministry of Housing and Local Government's Housing Manual of 1952, were slightly smaller than former post-war houses. Building work began on 14 September with contracts being awarded to T.R. Swann and Son Ltd of Sittingbourne and L. Edwards and Son Ltd of Newington. The first pair of houses took fifteen weeks to complete, and on 31 December 1953 the Principal Regional Officer of the Ministry of Housing and Local Government, J.E. Beddoe, performed the official opening ceremony. The completion of these first two houses marked not only the opening of a new estate but the beginning of a completely new outlook for Milton.

The housing programme was by now in full flow, and there was a definite need to clear away all of the undesirable and dilapidated houses that stood in the low-lying parts of the town around the Creek. In retrospect, it can now be seen that much of the local heritage was lost at this time as everything was demolished regardless of its age, importance or structural condition. With a little forethought and funding from appropriate bodies, much could have been saved and restored. A 16-acre former brickfield site in Staplehurst Road was earmarked as being suitable for the next estate, and once the roads and sewers were laid building work began in early 1955. This estate later expanded to cover the area of land once occupied by wartime prefabs and the meadow on which once stood the Meades windmill.

It was announced in 1957 that the 1,000th council house to be built since the end of the war by Sittingbourne and Milton UDC had been completed. The council had plans for a final 100 more houses but government restrictions on capital expenditure announced in 1958 cut the programme to just 56. By 1960, of the 7,000 houses in Sittingbourne 2,000 were council-owned. The 1960s was the final decade of the council's house-building programme and a final 500 houses were built by 1967 when tenants faced rent increases after a budget deficiency of £29,000. In 1973 the council

Bridge Street at the head of Milton Creek was another casualty of the slum clearance programme. *(East Kent Gazette)*

took control of Kemsley, the garden village created by Edward Lloyd, and by 1981 the houses were so improved that they were better than many of the newer-built council properties. In 1988 it was announced that in future control of council housing would be managed by a new housing association. The days of councils building houses were over.

However, the spread of housing developments continues through private developers who build on former agricultural land encroaching on the Green Belt. Estates both large and small are built wherever there is an empty plot of land regardless of its former use. It continued throughout the 1960s and into the 1970s, 1980s and 1990s. In the early 1970s, with house prices slowly rising, the council came under pressure to release more land for house building. It agreed, and in 1978 work began on yet another estate to the north of Milton known as Church Milton. It was declared open in 1985, but it was not until the early 1990s that some of the residents discovered their gardens were contaminated by lead and other dangerous metals. Unscrupulous developers had built part of the estate on an old rubbish tip.

In building new houses, both private and council-controlled, many old roads and streets vanished. As the new Mill Way carved its way from Sittingbourne into the industrial estate at Milton, most of the streets around the head of the Creek were lost forever. Similarly, when St Michael's Road was built many back streets of Sittingbourne were also lost and town centre development accounted for the loss of many more.

Swanstree Avenue, the start of Sittingbourne's proposed bypass. *(M. Clancy)*

Another section of Sittingbourne's ill-fated bypass at Homewood Avenue. *(M. Clancy)*

The Southern Bypass

By the 1950s the traffic flow along the A2 through Sittingbourne had increased at an alarming rate. It was felt the situation would get worse and a bypass was needed to get the through traffic away from the town centre. This was first noticed in August 1936 when a traffic census revealed that up to 960 cars per hour were using the High Street. By 1950 it had increased to 1,500, and by 1954, over 5,000. The government responded by building the M2 motorway. But in 1963 when the first section up to the Stockbury viaduct opened, it caused major traffic problems with 11-mile queues waiting to get on to the motorway during the Whitsun Bank Holiday.

Acquiring land upon which to build the Canterbury Road Estate provided a possible solution. On the far eastern boundary of the plot, Swanstree Avenue was built as the starting point. It would circumnavigate the estate before cutting through the agricultural belt and return to the urban area of the Ufton Lane Estate through which Homewood Avenue was built as a part of it. From there it was but a short distance across Borden Lane and back to the A2 via what is now Adelaide Drive.

Had the bypass been built, this is where it would have rejoined the A2 at the end of Adelaide Drive. *(M. Clancy)*

Borden Lane at its junction with Adelaide Drive during its construction in June 1964. Had the southern bypass gone ahead as planned after coming along Homewood Avenue, it would have crossed Borden Lane at this point and headed for the A2 through what is now 'Little Australia'. *(Mr Wheatcroft)*

The county council had carefully planned the bypass and Sittingbourne and Milton UDC accepted it with certain modifications, but subsequently it was abandoned and future attempts to resurrect it have met with strong objections. The fight against it continues to this day and is being fought by a well-organised action group. There are still tangible reminders of this bypass, not quite so noticeable in Swanstree Avenue, but obvious in roads like Brenchley Road, Capel Road and Homewood Avenue, where extra-wide sections of carriageway look strangely out of place.

Meanwhile, traffic volumes continued to increase enormously, exactly as predicted, and in 1973 a northern bypass had to be built from the A2 opposite South Avenue to Cockleshell Walk in the west. Discussions are now being held for a major new road to take traffic from the A249 Sheppey Way directly into the industrial area of the town then away to the east, through agricultural land to Bapchild, totally avoiding central Sittingbourne, but as usual there are several objections on many different issues. It will take a number of years to formulate a plan with which the majority will be happy.

Civic Change

Following the opening of the railway in 1857, a meeting was held in the Crescent Street public rooms to consider establishing a corn market in Sittingbourne. The new railway system had opened up a whole new way of transporting agricultural produce and local landowners were keen to use it to maximum effect. There was much debate with sound reasoning about where the new building should be. Mr Gordelier, who owned the Public Rooms in Crescent Street, thought his building should be extended for the purpose as it was close by the bank. Mr Knight of Bobbing argued that a new building in a field near the railway station might be more suitable, but Mr Dean objected, saying that property near a railway station was of little value in most towns. He proposed a site in the centre of the High Street. Eventually everyone agreed to this and in the following year tenders for the building were sought. The lowest quote received amounted to £1,090 16s 3d and work commenced; the foundation stone was laid by Mr William Lake in August 1858. The shareholders decided that market day in the new Sittingbourne Corn Exchange would be on Wednesdays, their first meeting being on 12 January 1859. The building was formally opened on 25 January 1859 with a Grand Concert, and in 1860 a triple-dial clock was added to the façade. The Corn Exchange was an elegant addition to the High Street but in 1878 it was taken over by the Local Board of Guardians who, after making improvements, reopened it as the town hall. It continued to be where the town's entertainment and public meetings were held for a number of years.

The council had grown considerably following its amalgamation with Milton and Murston. Its range of duties and responsibilities had increased enormously, but it never had a central council office. Different departments were housed in different parts of the

Before Sittingbourne's Town Hall was built, business meetings were held in the Public Rooms in Crescent Street, now the entrance to the Forum Shopping Centre. *(Fred Atkins)*

Originally built as the Corn Exchange in 1859, the building became the Town Hall some twenty years later. To its right beside the church is a row of shops later demolished to build Central Avenue. *(J. Clancy)*

town such as the clerk's and treasurer's departments, whose offices were above Burton's in the High Street; the surveyor's department was at Lydbrook House in London Road; the public health officer was based at Johnson House in Burley Road; and the housing department was based in another High Street shop. Clearly it was an unsatisfactory situation. Like the rest of the town the council had grown, almost unnoticed.

When Don Allen was appointed as the new town clerk in 1948 it was felt the time was right to review the town's future development. One of Mr Allen's first tasks was to convene a conference of the various public service bodies to discuss the development of a civic centre for the town. There was some undeveloped land between the High Street and the Avenue of Remembrance behind the town hall, and the borough engineer and surveyor, Maurice Lashmar, had drawn up an imaginative plan showing how the public services could be centralised. Other possibilities included bringing the police, fire brigade, education department, the bus company, inland revenue and the post office all into the one area. If space permitted, part of it could be developed as a recreational area and provide a replacement for the dilapidated swimming baths in the Butts. The plan generated considerable interest, but owing to restricted access and deployment the bus company, whose depot was at that time in East Street, and the fire brigade, already in the High Street next to the Baptist church, found the proposed location unacceptable.

Sittingbourne Town Hall on the morning that demolition began in August 1969. David Colthup happened to be passing, so he promptly sat down on the kerb to draw this picture. This is the only known front-on view of the building. *(Sketch by David Colthup)*

An access road had to be built, which involved the demolition of several properties between the United Reform church and the Town Hall. At first it stretched for just a few hundred yards and did not connect with the Avenue of Remembrance for some time to come. As office buildings became available, the inland revenue and the post office were the first to move into their new premises in 1961. There was already a new telephone exchange on the site serving over 2,200 subscribers, 850 more than at the old site in the High Street. In 1966 plans were announced for the installation of a further 800 new lines.

Station Street in 1974, before being destroyed when St Michael's Road and the Forum car park cut a huge swathe through it. *(Fred Atkins)*

The library had for many years been above Burton's in the High Street, but by 1951 was declared inadequate, so in 1953 it moved to a temporary building behind the town hall. The library we have today was opened in 1958 by author H.E. Bates, who told how his well-known work, *Darling Buds of May*, had been inspired from an earlier visit to Sittingbourne when he saw a family closely resembling the Larkins, complete with an old army lorry, in a nearby village. The new library cost £10,000 to build and in 1971 was extended at a further cost of £50,000. Milton's library closed in the 1990s and Sittingbourne's became the central library.

The council's next priority was to rehouse its various departments in one central building. When the girls' grammar school at Brenchley House in the High Street moved to a new purpose-built site in Highsted Road in the late 1950s, it released the old playing field, which the council added to the land they already held. The old Town Hall was demolished, and Central Avenue was at last widened and extended through to the Avenue of Remembrance. Work began on the new civic centre and finished ahead of schedule in 1965. The police began their own building programme to replace the outdated Park Road police station, which was later converted to become the magistrates' court, and in the 1970s moved into their new police station in Central Avenue. Meanwhile a new ambulance station opened in St Michael's Road in 1963,

In linking the new Mill Way industrial estate to Staplehurst Road and the A249 Sheppey Way, many old buildings were demolished, including the Grapes in Chalkwell Road. *(Fred Atkins)*

The New Inn, later renamed the Wyf of Bath, in Milton Road. The road to the left led into Wills and Packham's brickfields. This pub and the whole area were demolished in the early 1970s to make way for the new Mill Way. *(Fred Atkins)*

Trotts Hall after it had been rebuilt at Milsted. The building stood in Bell Road, Sittingbourne, for many years, but when its owner, Rex Boucher, foresaw imminent development of the area, he had the house demolished brick by brick and rebuilt at Milsted. *(M. Clancy)*

despite the road itself not being opened until the following year. The new fire station had to wait until 1981 before it could move from its High Street site next to the Baptist church. Maurice Lashmar's dream of a centrally placed civic area had been achieved, even if somewhat short of the original concept, with his characteristic energy and imagination. It gave the town a point of focus at last.

More changes came in 1973 in the face of major local government reform when Sittingbourne UDC amalgamated with those of Sheppey and Faversham to form the unified district of Swale. In 1977 it was granted borough status with the right to elect a mayor. As a new, much larger local authority it had new offices built on the corner of East Street and Crown Quay Lane, where in earlier times had stood a row of almshouses. The 1970s also brought changes that altered the face of Sittingbourne in a major way. Never before had such swingeing changes been made. St Michael's Road was constructed, running from Canterbury Road at a point opposite South Avenue to West Street. As it tore a path through the northern section of the rear of the High Street, not only were many historically important buildings like St Michael's vicarage and the Latimer chapel lost, but entire streets disappeared as well. With large industrial trading estates being built in Sittingbourne, Milton Regis and Murston, new roads had to be built for access. Much of the area around the head of Milton Creek was swept away as Mill Way was constructed to connect with Saffron Way. As a final act of indignity, the rubble from the demolished houses was used to fill in parts of the Creek. It was similarly so in Murston. Station Street, originally built to connect the High Street with the railway station was demolished in 1969–70. If a former resident who moved away say fifty years ago came back today, he or she would hardly recognise the town.

ELEVEN
A Personal Reflection

I am proud of being an Old Miltonian, having lived in the town since the early 1940s. For many centuries much of Sittingbourne and the surrounding area has remained unchanged despite the massive industrial developments that have taken place. Its High Street has stood solidly, but boringly, in testament to this for many years. Sittingbourne was never a town people visited for shopping or sightseeing. It just never seemed to make the most of its history or heritage. In the mid-1960s I married and due to reasons of work, moved to Gillingham. And there we stayed until I took early retirement in 1993. In the intervening years we hardly ever returned to the old town. On the occasions we did, it was usually by the shortest route to either parent's houses, bypassing the High Street completely.

When the decision was made to come home in 1997, we both eagerly looked forward to renewing our acquaintance with the old town once again, but what a shock awaited us. In the thirty years that we had been away the town had changed almost beyond recognition.

One of the first things that we noticed was that a new ring road, St Michael's Road, had been built to the north of the High Street taking through traffic away from the shopping area. After refurbishment work, the High Street was partly pedestrianised. After standing forlornly empty on the edge of St Michael's Road, the old swimming baths were demolished and replaced by the new Swallows Leisure Centre in the Avenue of Remembrance, which was opened by Princess Anne in 1989.

When constructing St Michael's Road, many back streets and old buildings were pulled down and even more vanished in 1980 when the Forum Shopping Centre, with its entrance in what had once been Crescent Street, was opened. Its shops were a welcome addition to those already in the High Street.

Most of the former brickworks had been built on by industrial estates, which seemed to link up and form an extensive vista of prefabricated buildings stretching across the northern part of the town. The Creek was no longer smelly, but little of it remained at its head. A new road, Mill Way, had been built to link Sittingbourne to yet another

Looking over the roof tops from the now demolished Cross Street/Station Street to the High Street. In the background the spire of the United Reform church and the cupola of the old town hall can clearly be seen in this sketch from August 1969. *(Sketch by David Colthup)*

industrial estate, and in passing by the Creek all of the old houses had been demolished and the rubble swept into the waterway.

For many years Milton had been the poor relation of Sittingbourne despite it once having been the most important part of the conurbation. It seemed as if no attention had been paid to it for many years. It started to come alive in the mid-1990s when a traders association was formed and the old medieval fairs, now known as the Saffron Fairs in recognition of one of the town's former industries, were introduced. At Christmas time streetlights are strung up and Christmas trees decorate the entire High Street.

Another innovation, introduced by the newly formed Milton Regis Society, was the reappointment of the ancient office of Portreeve. Clearly, all of his original duties had long gone, but the idea was to have someone to act as spokesman for the town. In the years we had been away, the Court Hall had been reopened as a thriving museum.

The Court Hall was not the only part of our history that was given a new lease of life. The Dolphin Sailing Barge Museum, the only museum dedicated to Thames sailing barges in the south-east, had been open for a number of years and was proving to be a major tourist attraction, as was the former industrial railway of the Sittingbourne and Kemsley Light Railway. In 1998 Sittingbourne at long last got its own Heritage Museum due to the perseverance of Cllr Peter Morgan. Five years on it is still housed in a former shop and has limited space for displaying the history of the town, but there are plans afoot to build a cultural centre in Central Avenue in the not-too-distant future.

New housing has continued to be built, ever encroaching on the last of our agricultural land. The latest sites are on the Meades and at Iwade, but despite offering more accommodation to more people, there is still an acute shortage of schools and other facilities. In the past much valuable archaeology was lost when brick-earth was being dug out. Today, before any excavation for building or industrial purposes can take place, archaeologists have to check the site. In this way, when new houses were recently being built in Iwade, a previously unknown Iron Age settlement was discovered. In October 2002 work began on building flats on the site of the former Sainsbury's car park near the corner of Bell Road and East Street. This was where Featherstone's department store once stood. During excavations, workmen uncovered some medieval foundations which are possibly the remains of the building that Featherstone's was before becoming a shop.

East Street itself is also under threat of being redeveloped, and if that happens we will lose the Plough Inn which dates to 1700. The White Rock in Canterbury Road is similarly under threat, which is a shame as it is the town's only example of an art deco-style building. Originally built in the 1930s as a nightclub, it later became the Labour Exchange before becoming a plant hire centre.

After a lengthy period of little activity, Sittingbourne and Milton have both come alive, and in the past forty years have started to develop and grow. The changes seen did have an advantage, as they gave me the opportunity to compile a collection of before and after photos, which was later published as *Sittingbourne and Milton Regis Past and Present* (Sutton, 1999).

Bibliography

Bellingham, Dr P., *Sittingbourne and Milton. An Illustrated History*, SAWD, 1996.

Brown, J.W., *Hasted's History of Milton Regis*, Local History Reprints, 1996.

——, *Hasted's History of Sittingbourne*, Local History Reprints, 1996.

——, *Ireland's History of Sittingbourne*, Local History Reprints, 1996.

Buckingham, T., *Sittingbourne Town Trail*, Sittingbourne Society, 1990.

Coles Finch, W., *Watermills and Windmills*, Arthur J. Cassell Ltd, 1976.

Cordell, A. and Williams, L., *The Past Glory of Milton Creek*, Meresborough, 1985.

Cordell, A., Lee, B. and Lee, M. *Sittingbourne and District*, Phillimore and Co. Ltd, 1989.

Deakin, W.H., *Sittingbourne and Milton Regis Conservation Study*, Kent County Council, 1974.

Feakes, L., *Woodstock, An Archaeological Mystery*, Geerings of Ashford Ltd, 2001.

Glover, J., *The Placenames of Kent*, Meresborough Books, 1982.

Grayling, F., *The Story of Sittingbourne Parish Church*, St Michael's Church.

Griffin, R., *The Lepers' Hospital at Swainestrey*, Local History Reprints, 1921.

Harper, C.G., *The Dover Road*, Anthony Treherne and Co. Ltd, 1907.

Inge, F., *Memories of a Sailmaker and Rigger*, Dolphin Sailing Barge Museum Trust 1998.

Midwinter, A.A., *The Church and Village of Tunstall, Kent*, Meresborough, 1992.

Monk, S., *Aspects of Farming in North Kent from 1570 to 1600*, Faversham Society, 1998.

Perks, R.-H., *George Bargebrick Esq.*, Meresborough, 1981.

Saffery, M., *The Milton Regis Trail*, Sittingbourne Society, 1994.

Scott-Robinson, W.A., *Sittingbourne and the Names of Lands in or near it. Their Origins and History*, W.J. Parrett, 1879.

Twist, S., *Murston Village and Parish*, Sittingbourne Society, 1993.

Twist, S., *Stock Bricks of Swale*, Sittingbourne Society, 1995.

Violet of Milton High Street, *Thriving Milton of the Past*, 1998.

Index